KING OF THE
SUNSET STRIP

ALSO BY STEVE STEVENS

So You Want to Be in Show Business

ALSO BY CRAIG LOCKWOOD

Surfing Yearbook
The Whole Ocean
Other Altars
The Other Game of Golf

As Editor:

Gangs: A Guide to Understanding Street Gangs
Surfing Rabbi

Theater:

Surf Story

KING OF THE
SUNSET STRIP

HANGIN' WITH
MICKEY COHEN AND
THE HOLLYWOOD MOB

STEVE STEVENS & CRAIG LOCKWOOD

CUMBERLAND HOUSE
NASHVILLE, TENNESSEE

KING OF THE SUNSET STRIP
PUBLISHED BY CUMBERLAND HOUSE PUBLISHING
431 Harding Industrial Drive
Nashville, Tennessee 37211

Cover design: James Duncan
Text design: Mary Sanford

Library of Congress Cataloging-in-Publication Data
Stevens, Steve, 1939-
  King of the Sunset Strip : hangin' with Mickey Cohen and the Hollywood mob / Steve Stevens and Craig Lockwood.
     p. cm.
  ISBN-13: 978-1-58182-507-7 (hardcover : alk. paper)
  ISBN-10: 1-58182-507-2 (hardcover : alk. paper)
  1. Cohen, Mickey, 1914–1976. 2. Stevens, Steve, 1939– 3. Criminals—California—Los Angeles—Biography. 4. Gangsters—California—Los Angeles—Biography. 5. Young actors—California—Los Angeles—Biography. 6. Organized crime—California—Los Angeles—History. 7. Hollywood (Los Angeles, Calif.)—History. I. Lockwood, Craig. II. Title.
  HV6248.C64S84 2006
  364.1092279494—dc22

                                                                    2006007336

Printed in the United States of America
1 2 3 4 5 6 7—12 11 10 09 08 07 06

To the comedy team of Yvette Fay and Lou Lowe.
Thanks for the laughter, as well as the tears.

And to my wife, Rosemary, for letting me
hang out with her—for more than thirty-three years.

STEVE STEVENS

WHEN YOU LOOK INTO A MIRROR,
MAKE SURE IT'S NOT YOUR EGO LOOKING BACK.

MEL STEVENS

CONTENTS

FOREWORD

Imagine yourself a budding Hollywood actor at nineteen, with an already-established career, living in post-War California in the 1950s, a place where glamour, wealth, and fame are as much a part of the landscape as the famous HOLLYWOOD sign on the mansion-covered hills above Sunset Boulevard.

Circulating in this heady atmosphere, as chance would have it, you meet a notorious gangster, Mickey Cohen, a real-life gang leader who is highly placed in West Coast organized crime. For reasons that at first you don't question, this gangster—who has seen you in several movies—takes a liking to you, and trusts you so much that he puts you under his protection and tutelage. Very soon you are accepted as a member of Cohen's inner criminal circle.

Trying to live in both worlds, you find yourself accepting the luxuries and perks that come with being a member of Cohen's gang: the expensive restaurants, the Hollywood night life, beautiful women, and more cash for running a simple errand than you can make in three days on a movie set. But it is a luxury you find laced with constant fear, anxiety, and ultimately danger.

Steve Stevens was just that: a real, live working Hollywood actor with dozens of television guest appearances and several films to his name while still in his teens and a graduate of a famous Hollywood preparatory school, with classmates such as Natalie Wood, Jill St. John, Connie Stevens, Bobby Driscoll, Annette Funicello, and the Mousketeers, as well as a long friendship with the young pop star Ricky Nelson. But somehow Steve found himself increasingly attracted to the lure of gang life with Cohen and the sweet, illicit perks that affiliation offered.

But the attraction of gang life had a bitter side: bloody violence, cruelty, an arrest, suspicion, surveillance, and contact with the LAPD, not to mention the fear of possible criminal indictment by the Justice Department.

This is a fast-paced, real-life drama that illustrates the simultaneously seductive and destructive nature of gang life's powerful forces, forces that can attract a bright, gifted, well-educated youth and then keep him, despite his close friends' pleas and concern, coming back for more until he finds those friends withdrawing because of who he is becoming, and he ultimately realizes how dearly he will be forced to pay.

AL VALDEZ, PH.D.
SUPERVISING INVESTIGATOR, ORANGE COUNTY
DISTRICT ATTORNEY'S OFFICE AND AUTHOR OF
GANGS: A GUIDE TO UNDERSTANDING STREET GANGS

ACKNOWLEDGMENTS

I wish to thank the following people:

Craig Lockwood, my writing partner, who pushed me into writing this book. He has known about this story for more than forty-five years, never judging me. He kept me honest and would not allow me to hold back my emotions.

Mark Stevens, my son, whose work and dedication on his screenplay *King of the Sunset Strip* helped in the overall development of this book.

Ron Pitkin, my publisher at Cumberland House, who had faith in me for the second time.

Steve Stevens Jr., my son, who had to double up on work at the agency while I spent time meeting my deadlines.

Mel Stevens, my dad. I'm so glad he didn't stay single. It's been one hell of a ride.

Ken Guran, for finding time in his busy schedule to scan photos used in this book.

J. J. Johnston, for opening the doors to his amazing gangland archive and sharing his scholar's knowledge and rare images.

Mary, our Lady of Perpetual Interrogatives, thanks again for a job well done. Bravo!

AUTHORS' NOTE

People and events in this story are portrayed to the best of the authors' ability to remember them as they happened. Where memory fails, imagination and perhaps a sense of humor suggested creating those misplaced names.

Researchers, historians, and people who know and write about Hollywood in the late 1950s and early 1960s should find that we have reconstructed that time and place with as much attention to specifics as was necessary to convey an impression—rather than smothering the reader in details—of just what *that* Hollywood and *those* times and personalities were like.

Forty-five years ago, Steve Stevens was a young man in his late teens, swept up in living these events while simultaneously pursuing his career in film. He had no intention of relating this story to anyone, let alone writing a book about it. Given the nature of what he saw and heard, it would have been both foolish and dangerous. So he kept no notes or journals.

Sequences of events, exact times, dates, and locations have gone through memory's filter, and since conversations weren't recorded, we have reconstructed them as best we could.

Were the criminal principals alive to dispute specific details of Steve's recollections, we suspect that they might. No doubt, certain individuals would suggest we, and you, the readers, "fuhgeddabout" the whole thing. But this is a survivor's tale, and Steve, the survivor, is now the only one—to our knowledge—who can relate it with reasonable clarity and emotional honesty.

Are these tales told "out of school"? No, that school is long closed. Its doors will never reopen. Think of them more as war stories. Any legal issues are now buried in the sands of time.

This isn't a true-crime "CONFIDENTIAL," and there is no effort made to expose, sensationalize, or betray anyone, or to smear people who have passed on and cannot defend themselves. Steve's is a survivor's account of a difficult passage from youth into adulthood, of experiencing the seduction of power and wealth, and of the price paid for even a brief encounter with its deadly radiation.

Steve Stevens is not alone among those in Hollywood attracted to notorious criminals. Several are mentioned in this book, and it is no less so today. But he is alone in recounting the experience. That's in part what makes this story unique.

Mickey Cohen was a tyrant-king and did what tyrant-kings do in their domain. His "boys" were his troops and they did what loyal troops do. And pied pipers of one kind or another have always lured youth in one form or another.

In doing what Steve did, he paid a price, accepted responsibility for his actions, and went on to live his life, and in so doing he enriched the lives of many, many others. In that way he differed from Mickey Cohen.

And while it is hard to imagine a criminal like Cohen—a "Public Enemy Number One," as the FBI once designated him—as a teacher or mentor, even a negative lesson can be an enduring and, in this case, important one.

Steve was recently asked if he had any regrets about this interlude, and he paused for a moment before answering.

"No, I don't have any regrets. I went into it with my eyes open. It was a lesson I was somehow fated to learn and, luckily, I lived to tell about it. The only regret I could possibly have had would be if I hadn't learned, hadn't gone on, met my wife, had a wonderful family, hadn't participated in so many talented people's lives."

STEVE STEVENS
CRAIG LOCKWOOD

In 1959, the notorious L.A. mobster Mickey Cohen and teenage actor Steve Stevens became friends—theirs was a sometimes humorous but often frightening relationship. This is a true story.

KING OF THE
SUNSET STRIP

1

THE DATE

I LOOKED AT the phone for the fiftieth time in the last hour. It was nearing five o'clock and still no call from my agent, Hy Sieger, about my next audition.

In Hollywood, careers are hung out to dry on telephone lines. I was beginning to feel like a has-been who never was.

Hy was a terrific agent—his claim to fame was discovering Marilyn Monroe—and he worked hard for his clients. I knew if he could nail me a part, he'd do it. But Hollywood's favorite game—played from studio exec to the lowliest extra—is the telephone waiting game, and the major chronic injuries as a result are either broken hearts from missed parts or osteoarthritis from perpetually crossed fingers.

I tossed the script for the play I'd been trying to read, *Waiting for Godot,* on the coffee table and pulled the last smoke from a crumpled pack of Parliaments.

I was a typical young bachelor. Shopping was something I occasionally forgot to do. My spiffy Hollywood apartment's kitchen cupboard contained half a box of cornflakes, a near-

behind HOLLYWOOD'S ★ ★ silken curtain

By
FLORABEL MUIR

HOLLYWOOD —Lots of new faces showed up at the "Merry Andrew" premiere here recently. All talented lads and lassies who will be seen more and more on the Hollywood scene. They are eager, willing and able to replace actors and actresses who are losing the race with years.

I saw Patricia Cutts, lovely English girl, who has a role in the picture starring Danny Kaye. Patricia was with Bob Evans, 28-year-old sportswear executive. Young Evans is torn between an acting career and his dress business and what do you bet the acting wins out?

New Singing Sensation

Ken Miller was with Kathy Nolan, the pert little trick you see on TV in "The Real McCoys." Ken has been stirring up a storm with his singing records.

Two teenagers, Steve Stevens and Marlene Willis, attracted a lot of attention. They are both bombarding the gates of cinemaland with everything they have, and I think such heroic efforts cannot long go unrewarded.

Tommy Ralls, who dances in "Merry Andrew," was with Sheilah Hacketts, assistant dance director on the picture.

Yvette Vickers, the doll who wears those startling dresses slit away down the sides, had one on that night. She was with Casey Tibbs, the rodeo champ of the USA. He wants to be an actor because "riding outlaw horses is not the easiest job in the world and doesn't promise a ripe old age."

Shelley at Movie Party

At a party in the commissary at the 20th Century-Fox studio after a showing of "The Young Lions," I encountered Shelley Winters. She came to the party with Red Buttons, who is still walking on air as the result of his winning the duke as the best supporting actor of the year.

Hugh O'Brian and Dolores Michaels are working together in "The Rope Law," so they came to the party together. Both assured me there is no romance. But who knows, by the time the picture is over there might be. That is how a lot of film love stories start.

Teen-agers Steve Stevens and Marlene Willis make cute looking couple.

empty jar of instant coffee, and five little packs of restaurant-pilfered sugar. The fridge contained even less.

But I never let little things like missing a meal get in the way of my success. Besides, the checks were actually in the mail. The kind you can count on.

On the plus side, my brand-new '58 Pontiac convertible's gas gauge was sitting just above the half-tank mark. Plenty of gas for tonight and making it to the audition I hoped I'd be having tomorrow.

But that was tomorrow. Tonight, I needed some fun. Some-one had once called me "a budding Hollywood star," and my date, Marlene Willis—who had been a class or two behind me at Hollywood Professional School, the studio-run private prepara-tory school for kids in film and entertainment—was a genuine "under contract" Hollywood starlet I'd recently run into at a casting call.

This was our second date in a week, and I was really looking forward to it.

Marlene was proving to be a talented singer as well as an actress. She'd not only recently starred in *Attack of the Puppet People,* but had sung the title song, "You're My Living Doll." And she was beautiful. Just the kind of starlet that any budding star—even one whose magnitude was somewhat less than stellar—wanted to be seen with driving along Hollywood or Sunset with the top down.

That took care of the first part of "being seen."

She wanted to see the new Paramount film *Some Like It Hot,* starring Marilyn Monroe, Jack Lemmon, Tony Curtis, and George Raft, about a couple of guys on the run from Al Capone's mob. Since it was playing at the Pantages Theater—on Hollywood Boulevard just east of Vine—I had that one covered.

"Mushy" Callahan, the former boxer, ran security at the Hollywood landmark. I'd scored some great autographed still shots for his niece of Annette Funicello from the *Mickey Mouse Club* show we'd both worked on, and I knew Mushy'd slip me into the balcony, gratis.

I had the first part of "looking good" wired. My old man managed an upscale men's clothing shop on Hollywood Boulevard, and I'd learned from an early age how to put together a great wardrobe. But the problem was affording the second part of "looking good."

Today in Hollywood, nobody's "broke." The euphemism's "financial issues." But in those pre-euphemism days, it was called "broke." And while I wasn't "broke" broke, I was experiencing a temporary cash-flow constriction.

I opened my walk-in closet and began searching the pockets of the twenty pairs of neatly hanging slacks. Bingo. A ten-dollar bill from the gray flannels. Another buck in the tan gabardines.

That'd cover things, but in those pre–credit card days, you had to flash cash, tip well, and hope Louella Parsons or Hedda Hopper—the major Hollywood gossip columnists—were watching you enter or leave.

On eleven bucks? Forget Louella and Hedda. I'd be trying to sneak past them on this budget.

Lady Luck, don't fail me now.

I began searching behind the sofa's cushions for more overlooked bills. But that bank was already busted. Even the dust bunnies cut and ran when they saw me poking around.

The truth was, despite my still-youthful looks, at nineteen I was growing older. Those age-limited parts were becoming increasingly less available. But there was a Hollywood Catch-22. Because of my still-youthful looks, the adult parts were a little beyond my reach.

Every kid actor knows the drill. There are only a handful of Mickey Rooneys, Elizabeth Taylors, and Jodie Fosters—more girls make the transition than boys. Fewer guys survive the cut. All too often, cute little tykes don't mature into handsome leading men.

I'd just watched a mutual friend and Hollywood Professional School alumni, Bobby Driscoll, who'd starred in Disney's *Treasure Island* and *The Boy with the Green Hair,* hit the skids and end up a junkie.

• • •

As I opened the convertible's door for Marlene, I was wondering where we could go after the film, when I felt something crinkle in the pocket of my sport jacket.

A few days before, I'd received a fan letter from a "Mr. Michael," inviting me to the Carousel—a neat little Brentwood ice-cream shop my classmates from HPS liked to frequent.

He'd written, ". . . you play tuff guys real good."

Well, maybe I did. Anyhow, I liked thinking so. So I'd stuffed the letter into my pocket and forgot it.

"Damn," I murmured under my breath. That free ice-cream letter was a hedge against my actor's temporary poverty. "Mr. Michael Who-the-hell-ever-you-are, you just saved my ass."

After the film I thought I'd try calling in another marker. Going to pick Marlene up I'd noticed that an old buddy, who was fast making a name for himself in rock and roll, was playing at a cool little nightspot on Sunset.

"Listen, Marlene, on the way over I noticed that Jet Powers is playing at the Sea Witch. Wanna try and catch him?"

"Are you kidding? Sure. He's great. I didn't know he was even in town."

Pulling out into Hollywood Boulevard traffic, we joined a solid, flowing stream passing between banks of Technicolor neon landmarks. The Broadway Building, Coffee Dan's, the Hollywood Theater, Zardi's jazz club, Goodrich Gym, Warner's Theater, the Iris Theater, Pickwick Books, the Egyptian Theater, Roosevelt Hotel, the London Shop, Grauman's Chinese Theatre, sweeping west into the warm California night.

As we pulled up, we could see "ONE NIGHT ONLY" splashed in red letters across the marquee—and a line snaking halfway around the block.

"YOU PLAY TUFF GUYS REAL GOOD." STEVE STEVENS (R).

"Oh, no," Marlene said. "Look at all those people. We'll never be able to get in."

"Well, he's a good pal, and I'll bet we can."

Pulling around the corner—luck 'n' timing—I found what was probably the only parking spot left for six long Hollywood blocks in any direction. If I hadn't impressed Marlene with my Stevens *savoir faire,* this little bit of Stevens *coup chance de stationement* was definitely doing the trick.

"It's a miracle!" Marlene cried with delight. And was it ever. There was still an hour left on the meter—and they didn't even check the meters after six p.m.

Holding hands—like a couple of teenagers in a B-teener flick—we all but skipped up to the Sea Witch and squeezed past the resentful-looking people in the line. As we reached the top of the narrow stairway, we were halted by the inevitable velvet rope and a well-over-six-foot 250-pound doorman/bouncer with not only bulging Gold's Gym muscles, but the Muscle Beach tan to go with them, and a resolute, don't-give-me-no-shit square jaw to match his flattop.

"Whadda you want?"

"Hey, champ, could you tell Jet his pal Steve Stevens is here?"

"Why'd I wanta do that?"

Translated, that meant: *Slip me a twenty, and I'll open the door and you can go ask him yourself.*

I, of course, didn't have a twenty to slip. Which left my next tactic—falling on his good graces.

"No kidding. I'm really a good friend of Jet's, and he'll . . ."

"Screw you, small time. Get your sorry ass outta here. You want in? Go stand in line with the resta the fuckin' chumps."

Now this was 1959, and by today's standards, Hollywood was still a very polite town. Nobody except the very vulgar, lowest class of individuals—probably drunk past redemption— ever used *that* word in front of a woman, young or old, without immediate—and often physical—repercussions.

Physical wasn't possible at five feet seven inches and 130 pounds. At least without going back to my car and taking the mitt off my baseball bat. So, that left charm.

"Now look, I know you don't know me from Adam, and you probably get a lot of people trying to worm their way in, but Jet's really a friend, and if you'd only be kind enough to mention it, he'll . . ."

"What? You're askin' me ta run your errands? Aw, outta here before I throw you down the stairs."

"Well," I persisted, "there's no doubt you could do that. I'll bet your day job's on the Rams' starting lineup."

"Rams, my ass. I wouldn't give you the chance to lick the sweat off my balls."

By this time Marlene—mouth open, red-faced, and unable to endure another word of the jerk's profane invective—was pulling me down the stairs. Probably a good thing. As stupid as it would have been—because I'd recently survived a severe head injury—I was ready to inflict whatever meager damage I could on the lout.

But the worst thing was listening to the angry crowd we'd shouldered through as they catcalled at us on our way down and back through their ranks. Talk about a lousy exit.

Marlene didn't say a word until we were back in the car. My shoulders were shaking with a combination of anger and embarrassment.

"I've never heard anyone talk like that, ever," she said.

"I have, but they were willing to pin a globe and anchor on me for doing it," I tried to quip.

She looked at me without understanding.

"They yell at you pretty roughly in Marine Corps boot camp," I tried to explain.

"Oh."

I started the Pontiac's big V-8, and let the rumble of my custom Belond headers and mufflers soothe my wounded ego.

"Hey, after all that, we need to cool off. How about we put the top down, cruise down Sunset to Brentwood, and get an ice-cream soda or something at the Carousel?"

I didn't know if that, or if anything at that point, would work to salvage the evening. But I was willing to take a chance. I liked Marlene; I'd liked her since we'd been at Hollywood Professional School, and I wanted more than anything to try to at least neutralize this disastrous evening so that we might have another.

Little did I know.

2

MEETING "MR. MICHAEL"

On Los Angeles's West Side, there are two "woods."

Westwood—in those days referred to as "the village"—was home of the University of California Los Angeles campus.

Brentwood—sandwiched between the main east/west arteries of Wilshire and Sunset Boulevards—served as the slightly rustic but very much upper-upper-middle-class suburb of Beverly Hills.

Brentwood—along Sunset Boulevard, which had a bridle trail running down the middle from Doheny Avenue west toward Santa Monica Canyon and the beach—had its share of estates, but it was a little less formal than Beverly Hills and was becoming a popular address with the up-and-coming TV crowd, who in the late 1950s hadn't yet attained either the financial or celebrity status they enjoy today.

Brentwood's little village square, where the Carousel was located, was out of the way enough for the general public not to know about it and "in" enough to be a great place to be seen by those who might like being "seen" without being seen.

That was a good enough spot for me. I parked and went around to open the door for Marlene. Maybe, just maybe, I could salvage the evening well enough to suggest we try another.

• • •

The Carousel was nearly empty as we strolled in at ten o'clock. We found a nice table, and I seated Marlene beneath the gallery of familiar movie-star faces in the black-and-white film studio publicity photos that lined the candy-striped walls.

When I showed my letter to the lady behind the counter, her eyebrows went up and she disappeared. A few moments later she returned.

"Hey, kids," she said, smiling, "whatever you want is on the house."

Thinking about my menu choices at home, and how little I'd actually eaten that day, I ordered their feature-sized banana split, which approximated the dimensions of a football. Marlene ordered a two-foot-high ice-cream soda.

In those days in Hollywood, young men and women didn't have to pretend to be sophisticated. Everyone assumed you already were. And so enjoying something as simple as ice cream on a balmy summer's night was, if not the height of cool, certainly acceptable.

Eight mouthfuls into the whipped-cream-and-chocolate-fudge calorie pile, I felt a kick to my ankle.

"Steve, don't turn around!" Marlene was facing the door, and her eyes were huge.

MICKEY COHEN AND JOHNNY STOMPANATO.

"Wha—"

"That's him, just outside!" she whispered. "I saw him on Mike Wallace's TV show last year. He's that gangster. The papers said Johnny Stompanato—the one Lana Turner's daughter put a knife in—was his bodyguard!"

I hadn't seen the interview Marlene was speaking of and, having been in the hospital at the time, barely knew about the April 1958 Stompanato killing.

Marlene shielded her mouth with her hand and whispered, "Lana's daughter Cheryl was just indicted for murdering Stompanato."

"Who's he?

"He's, like, a gangster who was dating Turner."

I half swiveled in my chair. Walking toward us, leading an English bulldog, was a stocky, dapper-looking little guy about my height with a round face and a semi-flattened nose, a wide-

JOHNNY STOMPANATO AND LANA TURNER.

brimmed Borsalino pulled low over one eye, and three serious-looking heavies. He stopped but didn't extend his hand. They stayed in his jacket pockets.

"I'm Mr. Michael. I sent you that letter."

This guy was a gangster? He looked like a producer. And there was no way his voice matched the Cagney/Raft tough-guy vocal style I—and America's moviegoing public—had come to expect. For one thing, his accent was more California.

The little guy turned to his linemen. Now, *they* looked like gangsters.

"Hey, guys, recognize him? He's the kid from that show."

The guard and center nodded. Their puzzled glances told me they didn't have a clue.

"So, Kid," he said. "I never knew if you guys really ever got those letters. It's encouraging to know."

"How d'you do, Mr. Michael?" I stammered. "Th-thanks for the letter and the ice cream. That was really nice."

He clapped me on the shoulder. His nails were perfectly manicured, but his clasp was like a pair of vice-grip pliers. My palms were sweating. I felt something on my leg and looked down. His bulldog was simultaneously humping my calf and slobbering on my pants leg. I thought about shaking him off and then looked at his neck and jaws. Nah, keep him happy.

"Aw, don't mind Mickey Jr.," said Mr. Michael, making no effort to pull the pooch off. "He's just tellin' you he likes ya. So, Kid, you play Hearts?"

"No, sir," I managed to get out. "Poker's my game."

"Yeah? Poker, huh? Well, that's okay."

He turned to the wall of flesh. "Somebody got a pen?"

He pulled a napkin off the table and wrote down some numbers.

"Whyn'tcha come over tomorrow night. You can even bring this pretty young lady if ya like."

For the second time in a very short time, Marlene's toe connected with my shin under the table. This time it was no tap. Between Marlene and the bulldog, I'd be lucky to walk out on my knees.

"That's really very nice of you, Mr. Michael. Thanks for the offer."

"No problem, Kid. Nice t' meet you both."

He turned and the two men stepped aside. Leading the bulldog, he walked through them, then they re-formed and all strolled out. All the other patrons in the place were staring.

Marlene pushed the unfinished ice-cream soda away and dabbed her lips with her napkin.

"Steve, I'd like to go now."

"But I haven't finished—"

"Now. Just as soon as his car's gone. Take me home."

"I don't get it, Marlene. He just treated us to this—"

"If I'd had any idea of just who it was that was treating us, I'd never have agreed to come. That man's an evil person. He's a gangster. And I don't want anything to do with him. Ever!"

I glanced longingly at my unfinished banana split, and split.

3

THE "TRUE GEN"

I FOUND THE near-empty jar of instant coffee, knocked some of the remaining powder loose, and spooned it into a semi-clean cup, tore open one of the last little packets of sugar, added that, and waited while the water heated. Leaning against the counter in my little utility kitchen, I stared down at the "to do" list on the pad I always kept.

The phone rang. "Steve, yeah, babe, it's Hy. Listen, I just got a call from your pal Steve Benson's mom over at Desilu. They're over at the Motion Picture Studio Center; well, that audition's been postponed until tomorrow. Catch ya later!"

Steve Benson was another youthful actor, and a former HPS schoolmate.

I'd begun harboring a suspicion that all Hollywood talent agents held secret meetings once a month. On the agenda were important procedural techniques like: Never let your client respond to bad news. Say: "Later, babe, love ya!" and quickly hang up.

For some reason, that call took the wind out of my sails. Another letdown.

Money was short, and that meant not having extra bucks for partying and hanging out at the bars that would serve a nineteen-year old. My actor's unemployment checks weren't due for a few days. I had enough gas to make it to the audition I'd planned to go on today, but not much more. That meant I'd have to limit any driving today to no more than a few miles, in case they called me tomorrow.

Shit.

I rummaged through the cupboards to see if there was anything I'd overlooked besides the stale cornflakes. There was a near-empty carton of questionable milk in the fridge. That, with the cornflakes, would cover breakfast.

Pushed back in a corner on the bottom shelf was a can of Campbell's soup and some crackers I'd overlooked. Lunch. Grim, but edible.

There were three cigarettes left in my car. I went out to retrieve them.

If I was careful, my Parliaments would last for what remained of the morning and the afternoon. That left tonight. Well, I'd worry about that when it came. Until then? Confined to barracks.

After what happened last night, I guessed Marlene Willis wouldn't be up for any more Carousel ice-cream dates. So much for romance. Given my between-pictures poverty, I couldn't afford her—or anything else—until my checks arrived. That could be—when? Hopefully tomorrow.

I thought about Cohen's invitation. It intrigued me that he'd invited me over to his house. Why? What did I have to offer him? Who knew?

Then that little devil that sometimes sat on my shoulder and whispered in my ear piped up: *But look at the bright side; at least it would be something to do.*

Naturally, the little shoulder angel countered: *But the guy has a bad reputation.* Hell, most gangsters had bad reputations.

But still, I was curious. What's someone like that really like? And suppose I took him up on his offer? What would I be walking into? A game of Hearts? Hell, I was safe. I didn't even know *how* to play Hearts.

My little copper teakettle was whistling, and I poured boiling water into the cup. Picking up the instant-coffee jar, I could see that there was enough for a few more cups. I'd just have to scrape it out and add a little hot water to the residue.

Then I noticed a case of unreturned Dr. Brown's Cream Soda bottles under the sink. A quick calculation netted me enough for a pack of cigarettes and a *Hollywood Reporter.* That'd get me through the day anyhow.

Damn. Why hadn't I remembered to go shopping?

I pulled on an old, comfortable pair of Levi's, found my sunglasses, slipped into my favorite pair of moccasins, and headed to the little grocery store down the street. I noticed a car belonging to one of my pals, an old Mercury woody station wagon, was parked almost in front of my apartment building. I looked around but didn't see him. That was odd.

By the time I returned, read the *Hollywood Reporter,* and smoked three more cigarettes, I'd burned up two hours. I nursed my coffee, tried reading Godot, and finally gave up. Boredom was getting to me. I went into the bedroom, lay down for a few minutes, got up, made the bed, and put away some clean laundry.

Finally the phone rang again.

"Steve, it's Lockwood. Hey, you probably noticed my car was outside your place. I was just leaving Anthony Mazzola's and my water-pump impeller went out. I coasted down to your block and left it there. I had to get back to school for midterms, so I won't have a chance to get over and fix it until tomorrow."

Craig Lockwood had been a class ahead of me at Hollywood Professional School, as had Anthony. The Mazzola family lived off Sunset on Ogden. The entire family had worked in Hollywood's film industry in one capacity or another since 1914.

Anthony Mazzola's brother Frank had played a part opposite Sal Mineo in James Dean's *Rebel Without a Cause.*

"No problem. I'll keep an eye on it. Say, maybe you can do me a favor," I said, and told him about what had happened the night before. "So, what do you know about him? Is this guy really a big gangster?"

Lockwood was studying creative writing at UCLA with Robert Kirsch, the novelist and book review editor for the *Los Angeles Times,* writing a college newspaper column, and had just started an internship at a weekly newspaper in Laguna Beach. He also worked part-time as a city lifeguard. His dad, Bruce Lockwood, had been an Associated Press bureau chief and a screenwriter for Fox.

"Cohen, huh? Yeah, he's pretty heavy, a real gangster, Steve."

CRAIG LOCKWOOD.

PHOTO: *LAGUNA BEACH POST*

VINTAGE COHEN, 1948.

"Was he tied to that Lana Turner/Stompanato murder?"

"Well, word was that Stompanato was linked to Cohen, but I'm not sure how. But let me see what I can dig up. I know a guy who works as a copy editor at the *Examiner* and another who's a crime reporter. I'll check and get back to you."

I made another cup of instant coffee, fished out my second cigarette, and waited. About an hour passed and the phone rang.

"Okay, Steve, this 'Mr. Michael' you said he's calling himself? He's a Jewish syndicate guy, a local boy, started out as a street-tough in east L.A.'s old Jewish section, Boyle Heights. He went back East and did knock-overs and stickups. He worked in Chicago with Al Capone's brother, and was sent back to California by the syndicate before the war with Bugsy Siegel to take over some rackets. He's pretty big-time. The Feds designated him a 'Public Enemy Number One.'"

"You're shitting me."

"Nope. That's right off his Federal Prisoner Report in 1952. Know who his attorney is? Melvin Belli. The newsroom down here has a lot of stuff on him. He's got convictions here in L.A. going back to 1933."

"Like?"

"Like robbery, embezzlement, assault, bookmaking, suspected murder, conspiracy to murder, assault with a deadly weapon. That's just the local shit. Then he's got a bunch of federal charges."

"It's hard to believe," I said. "What's funny is that he seems like such a nice guy. He's generous, loves to hear about what I'm doing. . . ."

"Hey, he's a real Robin Hood to some people here, Steve. Saved an old lady from being evicted by an unscrupulous businessman. Even went out to one of the juvie facilities in Riverside last year to talk kids out of crime. Don't think he was too successful. Didn't even manage to convince himself. Anyhow, in the end it looks like he's a pretty bad guy. He's probably rubbed out a few of his competitors."

Lockwood explained that the L.A. Police Department under Chief Parker and Mayor Fletcher Bowron wouldn't tolerate any incursion by organized crime from the East. What they *would* put up with, along with several local and state politicos, was a few homegrown criminal fiefdoms, especially those they could keep an eye on, and to some extent control and take an occasional cut.

"Steve, here's how that works. Right after the war, when there was an influx of population, the criminal syndicates wanted to move in and run things, but they had to be low-key and not piss off the LAPD. So they used a simple strategy. They started by having some of their trusted guys eliminate the heads of existing local criminal networks and take them over. That's how Cohen seems to have worked. He was one of those guys linked strongly to the mob on the East Coast. He took over the horse-betting rackets and, last year, all the cigarette vending machines."

"I always thought all that stuff only happened in New York and Chicago," I said.

"Well, yeah, sure, but we have our share of it here. Especially in Hollywood where there's plenty of money floating around."

"So how do they know who's who and what they're doing?"

"L.A. cops have a network of informants. And they aren't into subtlety. Informant tips them off and the detectives spot the out-of-town thug and grab him off the street. They take him downtown on some charge for 'interrogation and booking' and Jack Webb the shit out of 'im. Somehow they miss the booking process. Afterward, they dump 'im on the platform at Union Station with a ticket shoved in his hatband. I got that from Bobby Hall, the private dick that hangs out at Schwab's."

"Not exactly common knowledge," I said.

"You want me to go down to the *Examiner* and check their morgue? There's a shitload of stuff on their microfiche relating to Cohen and Senator Kefauver's Senate Committee on Organized Crime as well as the State Organized Crime Commission. They have all the results of the Stompanato inquest. You want me to dig some of that up for you? There's a lot."

"Sure, I guess. Well, listen, thanks for the intel. That's pretty interesting."

"Sure. Hemingway calls it the 'True Gen.' Semper Fi, and watch your six-o'clock."

4

"PROPER" INTRODUCTIONS

I STARED AT the napkin with *705 Barrington* scribbled on it. Should I? After all, Marlene had been adamant last night after he'd walked out—leading that damn bulldog and trailing his muscle.

Lockwood had given me some pretty negative backstory too. And yet, somehow, all those negatives were adding up to a cockeyed positive.

There was something about "Mr. Michael" that was interesting to me. He wasn't a big guy—we were about the same height—but he had a way of not letting that diminish him. He emanated a confidence that was somehow reassuring. He was stocky, walked on the balls of his feet, and had a kind of economy of motion that belied his small stature.

I stared at the napkin again and fished out my car keys. Hell, why not. It was a chance to see a guy like that close up. Study him. Maybe it would come in handy some day if I ever got a part like that. After all, Hy had mentioned that the studios had been buying gangster movie scripts lately.

I turned off Sunset on San Vincente into Brentwood Village and wound down Barrington, just blocks from the Carousel. Number 705 turned out to be an apartment building. No long driveway, no stone pillars, no iron gates with a Caddy parked behind or guys with snap-brim hats and sunglasses. Not exactly the kind of pad I'd imagined L.A.'s most famous gangster would be living in, but what did I know?

Walking up the cement steps, I stopped just before the last one. I had to force my clenched, sweaty palms to relax. And the little shoulder angel was singing an anvil chorus in my ears: *Bail out, now! Bail out, now! Bail out, now!*

Right.

I pushed the doorbell. And the door opened. As if someone

705 BARRINGTON.

had been waiting, just inside. Before I could stop myself, I lurched back.

"Yeah?" The voice and the guy were both scary. His heavy black eyebrows looked like they'd been applied by the Lon Chaney School of makeup design.

"My name's Steve Stevens. Mr. Michael invited me," I managed to choke out.

"Yeah, shua, get in," he growled. You could cut the accent with a knife. "We heard about youse. I'm Fred Sica."

Reflexively, I extended my hand, and probably visibly winced when his grip began doing deep-tissue damage. *Act, Steve, act. Be the kid tough guy Cohen's told these hoods you are.*

Sica grinned and half yanked me into the living room, still holding my bruised paw in his mitt. The room was enormous. Only slightly smaller than Grauman's Chinese.

FRED (L) AND JOE (R) SICA

I'd never seen an apartment like this. Obviously an interior designer had put it together.

Mickey, sitting at a card table, looked up with a warm smile.

"Hey, Kid, glad you could make it." He turned to the other men seated with him. "Now, this is the kid I was telling you about. One helluva actor. You should see him play tuff guys."

I tried pasting on a tough-but-amiable grin.

"This here's Joe, Freddy's brother," said Mickey. He was smaller, older, and, while still threatening, a little more polished.

"Say, don't he do that *Mickey Mouse Club* thing with Annette on the TV, too?" There was a chuckle from the gallery. One man stood up and walked to the bar.

"I would'n know," Mickey said, chuckling. "Mickey don't watch Mickey, but this here's Itchy."

"Itchy" was Manny Mandel. He nodded. In a room full of pretty-well-cast heavies, his Steve Allen specs, bow tie, and Ivy League–cut suit stood out. He was dapper.

"Over there's Joey D." Mickey swept his arm to the left.

Joey Di Carlo, behind the bar mixing a drink, nodded. He was a tall guy who looked like a villainous Zachary Scott, with a pockmarked face and pencil mustache.

"Whaddaya want, Kid," he asked.

"Rum 'n' Coke's fine."

Mickey's step-down bar area held everything. Rows of bottles, a soft-drink dispenser, cartons of cigarettes, boxes of Cuban cigars. Joey D. handed me a frosty glass.

"*Mickey Mouse Club,* huh? I'm not so impressed."

"It's a paycheck," I offered. Putting Mickey Mouse and "tuff" together in the same beat was beyond my acting skills. I probably looked about twelve to these guys, and was beginning to feel about nine.

"Easy way to make a buck, you ask me," he sneered.

It was a remark best left unchallenged. I stayed at the bar, trying to look like a tough but unassuming youth of undetermined age. In a room full of L.A.'s underworld, however, nobody noticed tough. I concentrated on the unassuming part. It worked. I stopped being the center of attention. Except for Mickey's dog. He approached my leg with anticipation. At least somebody around here appreciated me, smooth-talking canine love-object that I was.

Mickey, the Sica brothers, and the other two continued their card game for another hand. Hearts was a game I neither understood nor played, so I kept being tough but unassuming . . . and uncomfortable as hell. Mickey's bulldog had forsaken my leg.

Mickey suddenly slapped his cards on the table and stood up.

"That's it, boys," he said, heading for the bathroom. "You don't get any more a' my hard-earned money. Let's go eat."

They all stood up, waiting for what I would learn was Mickey's constant and obsessive ritual handwashing to conclude. In a few minutes he emerged from the bathroom, rubbing his palms together with a hand towel to dry the last vestiges of moisture.

"C'mon, Kid, you go with me and Joe. Like the Villa Capri? I feel like some pasta."

5

THE BOYS STEP OUT

Someone pulled up in an impressive and obviously customized Cadillac Brougham and opened the driver's-side door for Mickey. Joe Sica opened the front passenger door and climbed in beside him, motioning for me to sit in the back with the guy who'd driven up.

"Kid, meet Phil." Phil nodded. I nodded back. It seemed to be the best alternative to offering my good right hand to further physical abuse.

"He's the actor kid I told ya 'bout."

Phil disguised his lack of excitement about meeting a youthful celebrity impressively. His chin lifted slightly. I could do that. I lifted my eyebrows to add a note of respect. His brow wrinkled slightly. Good. We were communicating.

Mickey pulled out, and another black Caddy pulled up next to us with the other men. In both cars, everyone was wearing a hat—except me. Wardrobe notation.

I was beginning to warm to the situation. Here I was, a teenage actor, hanging with some of the nation's top underworld

figures. Just riding right up there with them like the coolest of cool film noir heroes.

"So, Kid," Mickey began, "you know a producer name a' Ben Hecht?"

Leaning forward, I answered, "Yes, sir, I do. I mean, I don't know him personally but, you know, through the business. He's Burt Lancaster's partner. Very respected in the industry."

I must have hit the exact right note. Mickey grinned broadly and nudged Joe Sica. "See, I told ya. Kid's connected," he said. "Well, see, you might not know it, but my life's a real shoot-'em-up. Even though it's true, nobody would'n believe it. And he's real interested in writing it as a screenplay. He's even looking for a big star to play me."

Sica reached over the front seat and tapped Phil. "Maybe he should get Clark Gable, huh?"

Mickey gave him a shove. "Aw, hell, he's too old and ain't good-looking enough."

We all laughed.

Mickey made an easy right turn onto Selma Avenue, and we pulled into the Villa Capri's parking lot. Four red-jacketed attendants rushed up and began opening the doors of both cars. I heard "Good evening, Mr. Cohen" at least six times. Conscientious. Apparently it was important to them for Mickey to believe he was having a good evening, and constant repetition would ensure performance.

I found myself wondering if they thought he'd shoot them if he didn't.

We all got out and waited for Mickey, who had stopped with one foot still in the car. He was looking across the street at a three-year-old Ford with a missing hubcap, buggy-whip antenna, and two guys in suits sitting in the front seat.

Mickey pulled his hat brim down, walked briskly over to the car, and leaned in the open window.

"Who're—" I started to blurt out. Phil shot me a glance. I swallowed the rest of the sentence.

Itchy whispered, "Cops. Cocksucking cops."

"Aw, shit," Joe mumbled. "I hope he keeps his cool."

Mickey was obviously engaged in conversation. He stood up, arm still on the car door's sill, and gestured toward us. Finally he turned, waved, and walked back.

"What'd you tell 'em?" Joe Sica asked, puzzled at Mickey's obvious delight.

"Tell 'em? What else? I told 'em to go find some real bad gangsters to follow and leave us good citizens alone." Tension broken, everyone laughed. Phil slapped Mickey on the back, and we walked into one of Hollywood's legendary restaurants.

Villa Capri was about as "in" as "in" got. Not a week went by that it wasn't mentioned in the gossip columns of Louella Parsons, Sheila Graham, Harrison Carroll, or Sid Skolsky—as they speculated about the doings of Frank Sinatra, Lana Turner, Bing Crosby, Rock Hudson, or any of a hundred other stars and studio types.

Frankly, in my present situation as an underemployed actor, the Villa Capri was so out of my league it might as well have been in Rome. But, as such, it was a perfect place to be seen by someone who might be thinking of hiring me for his next picture.

It was great to look successful, even when the night before I'd been less than flush, and tonight I was even less than less.

Walking in, Mickey slipped the maître d' what—given his reaction—was apparently a golden handshake. We were immediately led through and seated at a large table that overlooked the room. Smiling, the maître d' whisked a large "RESERVED" card off the table, pulled out Mickey's chair, and fluffed his napkin into his lap after he was seated.

I was still trying to look around without anybody noticing me, and I was having unbridled success. Not a soul bothered to make eye contact. Obviously the dimness of the room increased with the price of the entrées and wine. And boy, was this place subdued. It seemed as though the only light was candlelight.

Seeing Mickey, a couple to one side began whispering excitedly to each other. Not so a couple on the other side. It was obvious the acne-scarred muscular guy in the extra-tight-fitting black silk shirt was less than pleased and more than slightly drunk.

Mickey grinned and waved, as if he were a reigning monarch. Then he stood up, still smiling, to go wash his hands. Returning, rubbing his hands in a gesture I'd come to recognize, he was still smiling.

"That's him. That's Mickey Cohen," said the big guy's date. "Wow. They say he's got nine lives. All those other gangsters tried to kill him. Nobody can even touch him!"

Muscles was underwhelmed. "Him? He's no big deal, just a little punk. I could kick his ass with both my hands tied behind me."

Without breaking stride, Mickey's right arm shot out, cleanly

MICKEY COHEN—AN OBSESSIVE HAND WASHER.

extracted a magnum bottle from the ice bucket on the next table, and with a swing like Bill Tilden lobbing a tennis ball, caught the guy flat on the side of his head.

Muscles sagged to one side and dropped. His date, shocked, gasped and then started screaming. With equal efficiency, Freddy and Joey D. scooped the unconscious offender up and made a swift, side-door exit. Itchy, putting his hand over her mouth, lifted the woman like a pillow and followed them.

Mickey nodded a polite thank you to the dignified but astounded couple from whom he'd taken the magnum bottle, put it back in the ice bucket, seated himself, and carefully replaced his napkin in his lap.

I must have been standing with my mouth open, because Joe Sica tugged my arm and brought me back to the table. In moments Joey D. and Fred Sica came back in, took their seats,

"WE'RE JUST GOOD FRIENDS." ANNETTE FUNICELLO AND STEVE AT THE 1960 EMMY AWARDS.

and began studying the menu and ordering drinks. Conversation resumed around me, but I was still vibrating with unreleased tension from the seemingly casual violence I'd just observed.

• • •

Finishing the main course, Fred Sica finally broke my silence.

"So, Kid, tell me, youse ever fucked that Annette?"

I was definitely no stranger to vulgarity, and even my brief time in the Marine Corps had certainly given me a few choice phrases for my lexicon, but this one caught me as off guard as Mickey's champagne bottle.

Annette Funicello was about as virginal as an Italian Catholic girl should or could be. She was sweet, talented, and absolutely respected by the rest of the Mousketeer cast. Maybe some of the adolescent boys might have thought about it, but nobody ever spoke of it, much less made a pass. It would have spelled terminal doom to any chance of a career with Disney.

"Uh, no. We're, like, you know, just good friends. It's really professional."

"Aw, c'mon, Kid, you can tell us." Sica laughed. "Say, I'll bet he's dickin' her on da side, don'tcha tink?"

As we were finishing, Mickey stood up, left a hundred-dollar bill for the waiter, and slipped into the kitchen to tip the chef and busboys. Returning after washing his hands, he motioned us to our feet. Outside, he tipped each of the parking attendants a twenty.

Across the street the hubcap-bereft Ford was still parked. Coffee-cup lids and doughnut wrappers littered the dashboard. So much for the cops. Mickey Cohen had just spent hundreds of dollars, and I'd just eaten the best meal of my life.

Outside his place on Barrington, Mickey pulled over beside my car to let me out.

"So, Kid, ya had a good time, right?" Mickey asked, offering his hand.

"Yeah, it was great. I've never been there before."

"Well, you call me tomorrow. Maybe we get some more pasta."

Joe extended his big hand. It was time to bow out.

All the way home my little shoulder-angel voice was yammering about what a mistake I was making, and all the while I was reliving the most intense evening of my life.

Who had time to listen?

And maybe I should get a hat.

6
FOUNTAIN LANAI

DRAGGING MYSELF OUT of bed the next day was hard.

Getting to sleep last night after endlessly replaying what Mickey had done to that big guy—the casualness of his violent reaction—was producing two conflicting emotions in me.

Talk about conflict! On one hand, Mickey's response to the big muscle-bound guy had been savage and frightening. I'd been frozen for long seconds, unable to move. On the other hand, it was the kind of action almost any man has secretly wanted to take when confronted with a frustrating situation like that. Bam! Knock that drunken insulting shithead down! Dust off your hands and have your pals drag the son of a bitch out into the alley and dump him there.

Justice. With no repercussions. And Jack Webb and his partner sitting across the street nodding, drinking coffee.

Then that nagging little angel voice piped up. *There actually were two cops outside. That woman was screaming. Why didn't somebody do something? Wasn't that battery, or assault or something? Battery is a felony, isn't it? People sue each other for less, don't they?*

As an actor, I'd played parts where I was called on to act as if I were a kid behaving violently. But this was different. I'd just watched a similar part played out in reality, by grown men, on the set of Life. And my little angel was saying, *Think about that.*

And I was ignoring it.

At some level I knew all that. Even at nineteen, I was dimly aware that I'd always paid a price for my immaturity, my impulsiveness. But being young, and a little full of myself, I was unwilling at the time to recognize that it's all on credit. The bill always comes due later.

Overcome by introspection, I began thinking about food.

My Israeli buddy, Joseph, and his wife, Gurtie, ran the best burger joint in Hollywood, the Sunset Grill. Located at Sunset and Gardner, the grill was just west of my dad's former laundry business on the same block, where I'd worked as a kid and between parts while I was going to Hollywood Professional School.

Dad's laundry was long gone now, sold, and I was more than grateful. I'd hated folding clothes and making deliveries. Especially when someone would recognize me. It was embarrassing. They saw you on screen and thought you were rich. But what my ego really dreaded was running into one of my classmates from HPS while I was lugging some bundle of laundry around. Some of them really *were* rich. And could be equally snooty.

With Hollywood being the great big small town it was in those days, people in the business at every level knew one another. And the people who ran the businesses the entertainment crowd frequented knew them, from bit player to studio exec. And like any small town, there weren't a lot of secrets.

Joseph knew his cluster of Hollywood actors by name and the parts they played, their ups and downs, loves and losses, frustrations and triumphs. Because he was a guy who had seen his share of turmoil and suffering in the Middle East, he responded with compassion. When you weren't working, he'd let you run a tab.

Because of his generosity, people always paid him back when they got a part. Stiffing Joseph would have been unthinkable.

Well, I thought, easing up onto one of the Sunset Grill's stools, it's not the Villa Capri. But that's like a dream. This is reality. I'm on the cuff.

"Stevie! Good to see you; where ya been?" Joseph leaned over and thwacked me on the shoulder.

"Making the rounds. Not a lot of work, either."

"No auditions?"

"Had one the other day. Still waiting for a callback."

"Schmuck, you gotta eat. You can't audition or act good on an empty stomach. Say, you seen who's sitting over there?"

On the other side of the L-shaped counter was John Ashley. He had more American International Pictures leading-role B-movie credits than I had fingers, toes, and teeth.

"That's O'Dale Ireland," Joseph whispered. "Ya know him? He's a director—a nize guy. Got a good rep in the biz. You know the other guy, the actor?"

I knew Ashley; we'd met on a number of occasions, but he wasn't a close friend.

Neither of the two men had seen me, and Joseph gave me the high sign.

"You go on over there. They're talking business maybe? I'll serve your burger by them."

Moving over, I slid onto the empty stool. The timing couldn't have been better. Ireland was pitching Johnny.

"We're calling it 'High School Caesar,'" Ireland said, tapping the blue cover of a script he was holding. "Johnny, this'll be a great part for you."

Ever timid and retiring, I piped up, "Hey, anything in it for me?"

John looked up and flashed me his Colgate grin. He was a

handsome, youthful leading-man type. Not tall, but well-proportioned and athletic-looking.

"Dale, this is Steve Stevens. He's been pretty active and has some damned impressive credits."

Ireland shook hands and looked me up and down. "You have a head-shot and a résumé?"

I made a 9.9-second round-trip to my car and back and handed it to him. Thanks to my superb Hollywood-conditioning regimen—poverty cutbacks on the smokes—I hadn't even broken a sweat. Ireland thanked me, handed the script to Johnny, and excused himself.

John got up to leave. "Say, you feel like a swim at my place?"

Not wanting to let that script out of my sight, I nodded. "You still over at the Fountain Lanai?"

"They couldn't drag me out of that place." Ashley chuckled. "Follow me over."

Located at 1285 Sweetzer on the corner of Fountain and Sweetzer, the place was notorious. All you had to be was rich, single, and famous, and the rest was easy. Just like everywhere else in the world. But, of course, in Hollywood, "single" was both optional and flexible. As Ashley drove into the gated underground parking, I found a spot across the street.

Entering the lobby and walking through the patio, Ashley was greeted by smiling babes, waving babes, willing babes, anxious lustful babes, and mildly interested babes. Just being in his slipstream was a testosterone high.

John was easygoing, cool, and just a little blasé. Obviously the right combination. It was clear Ashley was from a different social level. Family money, probably, and all the perks that came with it. He had a casual, confident way of handling himself. Charm. And, wow, a pal like me.

Inside, Ashley's pad looked like the Beverly-Canon Theater

on opening night. Not large, but tasteful. Posters from his films, lobby cards, stylish modern furniture. The place was sleek, masculine, comfortable. It gave off a subtle message.

Drop in and get laid.

Handing me some trunks, he pointed to an empty bedroom. "Go ahead and change in there. My roommate just moved out. And if you think of it, I'll be looking for someone who's reliable and needs a nice place."

My little angel was positively cooing. *Jump on this, Stevie; luck and timing. And keep your eyes on that script.*

"Funny you should mention it, John, because my lease is up in a few days. What are you asking?"

The price he quoted was less than my little unimpressively located single-sans-pool-'n'-babes. I couldn't accept fast enough.

"Only deal is, Steve, you hang your posters in your room only," he said as we walked toward the pool.

"No sweat, Johnny. I'm functionally but not indulgently ego-oriented."

He laughed, turning back to look at me. I noticed he had that script under his arm. It was a great ploy. Everyone in Hollywood knows what a script looks like. And the Pavlovian assumption is—when you're carrying one around—you're studying for a part.

Ashley found an empty deck chair, adjusted his leading-man-style Ray Ban aviator sunglasses, and gave me a "Knock yourself out; I'm busy" gesture.

Jumping in, I did a few relaxing laps. When I finally pulled myself out of the water, Ashley motioned me over.

"Say, Steve, there's a great part in this for you if you don't mind playing a dork."

"Dork? Shit, John, I'm an actor!" I blurted out. "I'd get down on my knees and play a Munchkin."

Inadvertently I'd said it within earshot of the unemployed

A SCENE FROM THE *ZORRO* TELEVISION SHOW.

harem surrounding us. One umbrella away, a Sandra Dee body double waved me over.

"I saw you in *Zorro* and on the *Mickey Mouse Club* show!" she said above the poolside din. "You were really cute. What are you doing now?"

Flashing me his patented grin, Ashley leaned forward and whispered, "That's Sandy, and she has needs that seem to need attending to on a daily basis. If you get lucky, give me an hour or two. I'll let you read this when you get back."

Get lucky? I got very lucky, Sandy got less needy, and I got back—just in time to walk into the apartment and hear John on the phone.

"Listen, O'Dale, I just finished the script. Not bad. I'll do it. And I think you need to audition Stevens for the Cricket role. He's perfect. Good. In two days? Great. Yes, yes, I'll tell him."

John hung up, saw me standing there, and tossed me the script. "You hear that?"

"I got the audition?"

"You got laid, got the audition, got the pad, and got the script to study. Now get lost, and start packing before you get anything else outta me. I have a date tonight."

WEST SIDE WARM-UP

I'D HAD SO much excitement in the last three days that my hyper-activity meter was reading "recharge."

I'd packed a load of gear in the car, but I'd have to make a couple of runs to the Lanai. And my gas gauge was reading a hair over empty.

While my luck was holding, my wallet wasn't. Not only was I between pictures, as they say in Hollywood, I was between paychecks, at least until the mail came today.

Then there was the issue of food, or the lack thereof. And I wasn't about to go back to the Sunset Grill. Tab or no.

You don't work a lucky place twice. You have to let it cool down. I'd also been remiss in practicing my Basic Opportunism skills. In Hollywood you need to use those when you're cooling down your overabundance of good luck.

Reaching for the phone, I called Mickey.

"Hey, Kid, ya called just in time. We're all goin' over t' Panza's. Y'know the place?"

"Sure, La Brea and Fountain."

"Meet us there—forty minutes."

Panza's Lazy Susan was another current if far-less-formal "in" spot. Neat old converted house run by Ernie and Mollie Caringi and their son Steven, a bit-part player who'd somehow convinced himself he was on an Academy track. Steven scored most of his gigs—an occasional speaking line here and there—by picking up the tabs for producers and directors at his parents' expense and indulgence. I was a fairly consistent customer, and Mollie Caringi and the piano player, Art Thompson, always treated me as if I were a star.

Not son Steven. His indifference bordered on insult. When I walked in he looked like he was making his bid for an Oscar for "Best Display of Disdain in a Minor Role."

As I walked in, the *Mickey Mouse Club* song greeted me. At the piano, David Carlson, another Hollywood Professional School pal who'd graduated with Craig and Jock, gave me a wave and extended the vamp. David, who had opened Panza's piano bar for the Caringis, was sitting in tonight for Art. Dave gave one of his rich trademark keyboard flourishes and chorded out the last bar "M-O-U-S-E."

Son Steven grimaced as though I'd trailed in a shoe full of dog shit.

"Piano bar tonight, Stevie?" He'd started to crowd me toward a stool.

Stevie? "Thanks, no." I stood my ground, ignoring him.

To Carlson, I said, "Hi, Dave. Hey, I'd join you, but I'm supposed to meet a friend. I was wondering if he's here."

"And just who might that be, Stevie?" smarmed Steven.

"Why, Mickey Cohen," I said as casually as I could and keep from smirking. *Probably the biggest tip you'll get all evening, you unctuous one-upping sap.*

First Steven's brow lifted, then the eyelids followed, then the upper lip moved and his mouth dropped open. At the piano, Carlson threw me a puzzled look.

DAVE CARLSON AT THE PIANO.

"Certainly, ah, Mr. Cohen's table is, ah, right back here," Steven replied, audibly sucking in his breath. "This way."

This way? Right. Panza's wasn't that big a place. Dim, yes. But bright enough to see Rock Hudson on my left with his agent Henry Wilson.

"Hi, Henry," I said as we walked past. Henry held up the *Hello, busy now* index-finger signal. Just past him were Kirk and Mrs. Douglas. I gave a friendly wave, received a gracious smile.

Spotting me, Mickey gave me his big arm-gathering welcome and waved me in beside Fred Sica and a very sexy but sleazy-looking young woman.

"Kid, this here's Cookie. A stripper and a high-class dancer. Wait till you see her dance."

Cookie stopped chewing her gum with her mouth open long enough to squeeze out a "Hi."

"Hi, Cookie," I said trying not to focus too long on the Grand Canyon cleavage. Probably the point of Cookie's "dancing" was the stripping, which would probably start about four steps into the "dancing."

Mrs. Caringi came up with a covered dish on a tray, and patted my shoulder. "Steve, take a whiff. I just made this for Mickey—special!"

Mickey's eyes widened as she lifted the dish's cover and the rich aroma wafted out. Son Steven appeared.

"Everything all right here? Anything for you to drink, Steve?"

"Steve"? Okay, we dropped the diminutive. Making progress. But the "Anything for you to drink" was code for "You're too young for booze, and we both know it, you little jerk."

"No, thank you," I said ultrapolitely. "Unfortunately, I'm not yet twenty-one." Meaning: *And I've got way more credits and a lot bigger career than you have and you're ten years older, and still working as a waiter—chump!*

"Aw, bring him a Coke." Mickey waved him away. Abashed, Steven took a step back and did his best to look down his nose at me.

"That'll be fine, Stevie," I said. *Now who's the "-ie"?*

"Coming right up, Mr. Cohen," he replied. A lame attempt to salvage his dignity.

Payback, Stevie, I thought. This was becoming sweet revenge.

Mickey punched my shoulder. "So, what'd you do today, Kid?"

"Scored an audition for a new picture, and started moving."
I didn't mention the quickie. Mixed company.

"Picture, huh," Mickey said. "Another tough-kid role? Jeez, Fred, ya gotta see how this kid plays tough guys."

"Funny you should mention it, Mr. Cohen. The title's *High School Caesar*, but I play the exact opposite in this movie. I'm a wimpy kid, the one the tough guys work over."

Mickey looked disappointed. "So, what you tellin' me? You playing a wimp? Aw. I like tuff kids. Reminds me a' me."

"It's a pretty good part," I said defensively. "And the guy I'm moving in with, John Ashley, plays the lead."

Cookie's breas—er, eyes—perked up at the mention of "part" and "Ashley."

"You? Movin' in with John Ashley? I looove him. Where's he live?"

"Fountain Lanai," I said, working hard on not sounding too impressed with myself. It *was* one hell of a step up.

Magic words, apparently. Cookie had a tectonic mammary shift. Another pneumatic inch of flesh suddenly escaped from her none-too-secure low-necked dress. It's a good thing she hadn't noticed Rock Hudson or Kirk Douglas in the other room. That might have resulted in a breakout of—"dancing."

"So, you know Mama and everyone here already?" Sica asked.

I nodded.

"He's real Hollywood, this kid, a local," Cohen said, patting my arm. "You know where I grew up?"

I shook my head.

"Boyle Heights. The old Jew section, across town, east L.A. They din't eat in places like this."

"My dad spent some time there. Now he says it's turning Mexican."

"Turning? Ha-ha, you could say that." Mickey laughed. "So, where's the old man from?"

"Originally? New York. Down in the Bowery. He was an orphanage kid. Hung out with the Italian kids. Said they were so tough and dirty that when they swam in the East River they left a ring around the pier."

"Ha-ha, 'at's terrific—I love it!" Mickey's approving chuckle and smile spoke volumes. "I thought because of your moxie you weren't no California kid. You been to New York?"

MICKEY COHEN, BOXER.

"I was born there. My folks moved us out here from Benson-hurst when I was little."

"Who don't know *that* neighborhood? Y'know, I fought professional all over the East Coast—back in the thirties. Chicago, Cleveland, Philly, New York. Everywhere."

"Professionally?"

"You din't know Mickey was a boxer?" Sica pointed with his fork. "Now, this man could show you some *real* tough-guy moves."

"You really boxed professionally?" I said, probably sounding as impressed as I actually was. Boxers—especially the professionals in those days, before martial arts and flying kung-fu artists like Chow Yun-Fat—occupied a position of awe and respect in the minds of most younger men.

Mickey wasn't big, but he was solid. And I'd noticed how easily he moved. When he spoke to you his eyes stayed on you, *lock-on-target,* as they say in the Corps.

Dinner over and Mickey's usual largesse in tips distributed, hands washed, with nods, waves, and good-byes said, we waited for the valet to bring up Mickey's big Cadillac Brougham. Approaching us from across the lot was a big guy who stopped before Mickey, and respectfully extended his hand.

"Mr. Cohen, I'm Max Baer Jr. My dad speaks highly of you."

Mickey laughed. "Now there's a name. Max Baer, the Livermore Larupper from Livermore, right here in California. A great fighter."

Anyone who knew anything about boxing knew that Baer had been a heavyweight champion, beating Max Schmeling, the World's Champion, in New York in 1933. His son took a different path, eventually starring as Jethro on *The Beverly Hillbillies.*

"Yeah, a great fighter, your dad. You tell him Mickey says hello. And tell him I think you got too pretty a face to follow the old man inta the ring. You got the looks. Be like this kid, be an actor. We're going to take in a coupla clubs. You should join us."

Baer laughed and politely declined, and soon we were headed south down La Cienega Boulevard where West Hollywood's best steak houses like Lawry's Prime Rib alternated with exclusive art galleries and high-end antique shops.

Sitting in back again next to Fred Sica—but now with a full belly—I relaxed, staring comfortably straight ahead. It was a curious feeling. I'd somehow been fully accepted by a man I was learning was anything but a stock character and who had been labeled "an underworld figure" in real-life's casting call.

For whatever reasons, Mickey Cohen was treating me as though I were some recently arrived nephew or younger cousin. He was obviously rich, very obviously powerful in a way I'd never encountered in my brief years, and with him I was under an umbrella of power. And—since my little angel voice had signed off for the night—it felt good.

But while my eyes were elsewhere, I couldn't help but hear their conversation. Something was troubling Mickey, somebody named O'Hara.

"He seen ya walking Mickey Jr. and he said what?"

"He said, 'So yer walkin' Mickey's dog. Wha's 'at, a promotion?' Then th' bastid drove off."

"An' you didn't shoot him? Fuckin' shitheadcocksucker. I'da shot him."

"Aw, fuhgeddaboutit, Mickey, fer Chrissakes," said Fred at one point. "Jack O'Hara's nuthin' but a rich-kid punk. A nuttin'. Don' worry. It'll be taken care of."

I'd seen enough gangster movies to know that "taken care of" didn't imply being comfortably settled in a nice apartment in the Park La Brea Towers with a trust fund. These were real gangsters talking real gangster talk, and O'Hara, whoever he was, was being described in the future indicative tense. Never a good thing.

I kept staring. Straight ahead. No longer relaxed.

8

LA CIENEGA LAUGHS

We pulled up in front of the Slate Brothers comedy club, run by two former comics and still-working actors. This was one of those spots where popular comedians would come to try out and refine new material, while newer comics could showcase their acts.

A cluster of red-jacketed car valets swarmed up, opening the doors and proclaiming, "Evening, Mr. Cohen, sir," as though they were announcing arrivals at a Grauman's Chinese Theatre opening for a major feature.

"Kid," said Mickey, smoothing out his suit and passing out tips, "go see if you can get us a table, huh?"

I didn't actually say, "Yes, sir, yes, sir, three bags full." But I sprinted.

Blocking the door to the club was a guy who was only slightly smaller than King Kong. But not nearly as attractive.

"What're you, fifteen?" he said. "Go backta kindergarten, punk. You ain't goin' in there."

"Uh . . ." I hesitated, completely stymied by his attitude and bulk. "I'm with my, uh, uncle."

"Your uncle? Like who's your uncle, schmuck?"

"Like? Like he's not Uncle Schmuck, he's Uncle Mickey Cohen," I said, pointing back over my shoulder toward the parking lot.

"Oh, yeah, *that* uncle. Sure, okay, sorry." And as if by magic the doors opened as Mickey and the boys approached.

"Mr. Cohen, sir! Your nephew's got it all arranged," he said, smiled at me, and led us into the club.

"My nephew?" Mickey shot a quick glance at me, and his smile broadened. "Yeah. He takes good care a' his Uncle Mickey."

Inside, Mickey shook hands with Henry Slate and waved at the stage as Slate led us to a front-row table.

Onstage was a short, beefy-faced, stubble-headed guy who was doing his best to embarrass his audience.

"So, sweetie—yes, darling, you with Irving with the cigar that looks like a dog turd—a mink in this weather? Oy! Why don't you just hang a sign around your neck that says 'Jew-ish'!"

Looking at Mickey and Joe Sica, he took a puff off his cigarette and rolled his eyes.

"Jesus H. Christ, it's Hollywood's most lovable hoodlum. Tell me, already, you guys lost? Forget the road to Vegas? So, Mickey, make yourself at home; shoot someone."

I could see Fred Sica stiffen. Mickey, on the other hand, had started to double up.

Rickles leaned forward with the mike stand pointing at Sica. "What's this, the Mafia overflow? Mickey, I swear, I paid my bookie. Shouldn't he be out putting someone in cement shoes? Where's the fuckin' Kefauver Committee when you really need them?

"Mickey, you know I don't mind you, sweetie, but where'd you find this riffraff?

"And this broad? Her tits are bigger than two Holsteins'. Honey, find someone your own species. By the way, what is your nationality? I know, I know, it's a big word. Stretch. Bovine, maybe?

"Mickey, is this her date? Has he had his shots? Kid, is Mickey gonna set you up with a vegetable stand? Who picks out your clothes, Ray Charles? You got a building permit for that pompadour? Turn around; let me see the back. What, you didn't get a haircut on purpose or you're hiding a dirty collar?"

Don Rickles, "Mister Warmth," as he was starting to be referred to in Hollywood, was the master of put-down comedy. Nothing was off-limits—race, religion, sex, age, economic status—nothing. And while Mickey and I had loved it, Cookie didn't get it, and Sica kept shaking his head, unable to fathom how the ordinarily touchy and quick-to-take-offense Mickey found Rickles funny.

Wrapping up his set, Rickles strolled over to the table. Mickey introduced Sica, who clearly hadn't been amused and looked as though he was about to pull out his piece and begin pistol-whipping the irreverent little comic. There was a long moment while Rickles's hand hung suspended before Sica reluctantly took it.

"Don, meet Steve Stevens. He's on the *Mickey Mouse Club* show on TV."

"So, Mickey's running with Mickey? I gotta remember that one."

"And Steve? You're working on keeping Mickey away from bad influences? He's gonna be so wholesome by the time you're done with him that Billy Graham'll volunteer him for the Mormon Tabernacle Choir."

"Anyhow, Mr. Rickles, I liked your part in the sub movie." Rickles had played a submarine crewman in *Run Silent Run Deep,* the first of many film parts to come. Rickles rolled his eyes.

"Yeah, yeah. I spent three years in the Navy, auditioning. I flushed toilets and went 'PING—PING.'" Rickles was just as funny offstage.

Mickey stood up, nodded at Sica, and went off to wash his hands. Sica handed me the valet stub and inclined his head toward the door. Outside, I handed the stub to the reigning red-jacket.

"Mr. Cohen's car, please."

His eyebrows did a fast lift. "Yes, sir! On the double, sir."

And he sped off, leaving me with a curious feeling. If I'd pulled up in my brand-new convertible, gone in and come out, I'd have been just another young customer with an okay car, maybe worth a two-bit tip. But now, I was connected to Mickey Cohen. Red Jacket knew it, and I was just beginning to realize what that meant.

Mickey appeared, distributed a handful of twenty-dollar bills, and we headed toward Brentwood.

Mickey was still chuckling when we pulled up outside his apartment. "Freddy, the guy's a riot. We're in classy company, I'm tellin' ya. He gave Sinatra a load of shit the other night. He's got balls bigger'n pumpkins."

"Too big, ya ask me."

"You? You couldn't tell a joke if you could remember one."

"All I can remember is he crossed d'line."

"What about you, Kid?"

I was on the spot for an opinion. Of course I'd found Rickles funny. But I had also found myself wondering uncomfortably if his humor might offend Mickey or Fred and result in something like last night's champagne christening. I erred on the side of caution.

"Funny? Yeah, some things are a laugh, but the personal stuff, hell, I'm not so sure he shoulda used you. I mean, what if he'd pissed you off?"

Fred turned to Cookie, but Cookie'd turned in. She was asleep, mouth open, gum on the end of her small pink tongue. Mickey had to wake her up to take her upstairs.

Sica called me a cab. "Ya want something to drink before he gets here?" He actually sounded friendly.

"Nah, but thanks. I'm tired, and I still gotta drive home. Maybe a rain check."

Sica extended his hand, looked me in the eye, and said: "You're all right, Kid. Ya handled yourself okay."

9
MICKEY'S BIRTHDAY PRESENT

A DAY LATER, and I was stuffing scavenged cardboard cartons from Ralph's supermarket with what remained of my gear for a final run to the Lanai.

Doing a quick spot check, I saw the last thing in the place, sitting on my living room table—the script for *High School Caesar*.

Taking a break, I picked up the script. The part I'd be auditioning for, "Cricket," was something of a challenge. The kid was a bookish dork, a trusting friend of John Ashley's character—a manipulative, unsupervised rich kid who was into a series of high-school rackets. Cricket, because of his loyalty and naïveté, was suckered in deeper and deeper.

Flipping through the pages again, I started to look for a physical model, some series of characteristics that I could anchor my character in. Jerry Lewis's character in *The Sad Sack* offered me a few hints. I stood up, walked around, and repeated a few lines, imagining how Lewis might have played it.

Too broad. I had to go for some of the physicality, but my template had to be based in the character's pathos, his emotional neediness and desire for acceptance.

Reality was psychologically mimicking art, right there in front of me, but I was missing all the broad cues, all the not-so-subtle flags, and dispatches from the front. This character, Cricket, was a synchronous metaphor for my life—for this fascination with Mickey Cohen and what he represented—but I couldn't even begin to see it. I was creating a "role" in my relationship with Mickey that would allow me to gain some element of acceptance and approval.

But there was another factor I would fail to see, or even begin to understand. Psychological dependence works both ways.

• • •

Around four that afternoon the phone rang.

"Hey, Kid, come on over. You feel like some pasta, or what?"

Throwing the last box into my car, I went back in, took a final shower, tidied up, and put on some slacks and a sport coat. As insurance, given the last two nights, I stuck a necktie in my jacket pocket.

• • •

When I arrived at Mickey's on Barrington around six, Fred Sica opened the door. His brother Joe was making a call in the bar. Mickey Jr. lost no time in showing his esteem by humping my leg.

Mickey emerged in an expensive and well-tailored suit, wafting a cloud of cologne.

"It's my birthday, and I'm gonna buy me a nice birthday present," he announced, not stopping but heading straight for the front door.

Mickey's big Brougham was in the driveway. Mickey

motioned for me to sit in back, and I took a corner opposite Joe. No sooner had the car started than last night's topic was being aired.

Whoever this O'Hara guy was, whatever he'd done, he was getting top billing. And once again I was overhearing what was beginning to sound like a bad plotline for a B movie. Hell, I thought. Maybe that's just what this is.

I studiously kept my eyes on the passing scenery, becoming increasingly convinced that this was like some kind of club or fraternity initiation. Let me hear this stuff, dink me along, add a few details until they got a reaction out of me and saw what kind of guy I was. Like I even knew. Me, a nineteen-year-old actor?

Just south of Sunset on Vine Street, Fred turned into the Clarence Dixon Cadillac Showroom driveway, and we all got out. Inside, behind the towering plate-glass windows on the polished showroom's floor was the most incredible black Cadillac sedan I'd ever seen.

Mickey, transfixed, gave it a long, appraising look, while Joe, Freddy, and I began slowly circling it, Fred letting out a long, low whistle as though he'd just walked into his bedroom and found his ultimate sexual fantasy reclining nude and available on the bed.

Fins like a V-2 rocket, dual-headlights buried in smoothly molded overhanging chrome-accented eyebrows, a massive chrome grille and bumper structure with two enormous black-capped chrome protrusions that looked for all the world like Cookie's tits in a black bra, wide spoked wheels with racing-style knockoff hubs, dual exhausts, tinted glass, upholstered in Moroccan leather so soft and supple it felt like a pair of ladies' evening gloves, with chrome accents on the dash, and last, capping it like a silver crown—a solid chrome roof!

If Detroit had ever had an automotive industrial wet dream, this was it.

"I hear Sinatra has one," Mickey whispered reverently. "This is class!"

A well-dressed young salesman approached, but before he could say anything, Mickey held up his hand.

"I want this one. I wanna drive it outta here. How much?"

"Sir?"

"This one." Mickey caressed the fender. "How much?"

Behind him another, older man appeared, a fresh carnation in his lapel, and took the younger salesman's elbow. "I'll handle this. See if you can find Mr. Cohen one of our new complimentary windbreakers."

"I want this one, and I wanna drive it right off the floor. Tonight," Mickey said.

"We'll sign the papers right now, Mr. Cohen, and I'll order it immediately."

"Immediately? What's wrong with right now. My money's no good?"

"Mr. Cohen, not only is your money good, but when I saw you arrive I called Mr. Dixon. He's personally arranging a special deal, just for you. He'll be calling in just a moment to speak with you."

"But it's my birthday, I wanna take it now."

"And would that I could have you drive it right out. Unfortunately, this model Cadillac is the factory's concept car. This just arrived from the big auto show. The actual production model will have the new 450-horsepower engine, which I'm sure you'll find both more powerful and preferable. We're taking orders. Mr. Sinatra has ordered the first, and I'll assume you're going to be our next?"

Young Ralph's heels clicked on the marble showroom floor as he approached. "Mr. Braden, it's Mr. Dixon for Mr. Cohen."

The older man guided Mickey back to an office, and in ten minutes Mickey reappeared.

"I just spoke with Dixon. I was right. Only other one like

this is for Sinatra. The real ones are arriving next week. He says I'm such a good customer, buying new every year, and as it's my birthday, he's just called Ciro's. He made us reservations."

Mickey turned to Joe. "We're gonna have to make a pickup first. I'm payin' cash in the morning."

10

THE PICKUP

Mickey pulled the Brougham out of Dixon Cadillac and headed east, down Sunset.

There was no question that Mickey knew L.A. well and could find his way around with no trouble, but Joe and Fred Sica seemed a little less clear on the location of this particular debtor, who apparently had moved. It was beginning to sound like a slapstick version of Abbot and Costello's "Who's on First?"

JOE: So, Mickey, turn right, right here!
MICKEY: Right? Okay. Right.
FRED: Nah, nah, I meant left. Da joint's on anudda street.
MICKEY: He ain't at the store no more?
FRED: Nah, wait a second; nah, hold on. Le's see. Go, uh, go lef' at dis corna.
MICKEY: Okay, left on Vista Rio.
JOE: Up here, ya gotta turn, uh, no, keep on this side where the street splits.

FRED: That's, like, North Oilyveera Terrace; we need South.
MICKEY: Can't you even say O-lay-vea-ra, you dumb wop?
JOE: Vera schmera. I don't like Mex food, either.
MICKEY: What the fuck. There's the old store, over there. This is good. Wherever he is, they'll know. Go on, go up the stairs on the side a' the dump. Ask for Sobrano."

Hollywood Professional School's preppy teenage local lore had stigmatized this heavily Hispanic section of town around Chavez Ravine as something like East Berlin. Probably because of that, it was looking scary to me. It was obvious from the residents' faces that we were in the minority. But at least I didn't see a single pachuco chica with razorblades in her teased hair. So much for urban myths.

Fred returned. "Some guy says he's over in Boyle Heights."

Mickey shrugged. "This guy owes me, a long time. I hope we don't gotta teach him a lesson."

Turning around and heading back to Los Angeles Street, we crossed the L.A. River and climbed up into Boyle Heights.

This was another section of town I'd never visited. A place you'd normally try to avoid if you didn't have some specific reason to go there. Back in the early part of the century, it had been a nice lower-middle-class neighborhood. Over the years it had changed. Now it was almost exclusively poor and Mexican. And to me, that meant gangs.

None of the other occupants in the car seemed concerned. And finally we pulled up beside a small neighborhood grocery store off Soto Street. Fred exited, and in a few minutes came back holding a paper bag.

"Hows come ya din't tell me da guy's got hafa face?"

"Aw, he got it in the war or sompin'. Fighting for the right to play the ponies, right? I give a shit. Lemme see the bag."

Mickey peeked in, looked up, and smiled. "Paid in full. Now let's get outta here."

Mickey hung a big U-turn, came to a full stop, and entered an intersection when the light turned green.

Suddenly there was a screech of brakes from a rickety old produce truck and a jarring bump and sudden belching of steam as it ran the red light and collided with us.

"Shit, goddamn!" Mickey exploded, turning around in the front seat to look behind him. "There goes my goddamn trade-in."

Everybody climbed out to check the damage—only to find that the Brougham's bumper was unmarked. The produce truck's radiator, however, was deeply dented, leaking water, and hissing dying gasps of vapor.

Emerging from the truck's cab was a very old Mexican man with a large white mustache, and his equally antique wife.

"Senor, senor, los siete, mucho, porfavor. Mi camionetta es muy Viejo."

All of which went over all our heads. No one but Mickey spoke more than a word or two of Spanish.

Fred, with probation hanging over him, was conspicuously looking over his shoulder. "Mickey, let's get outta here before the cops come."

Ever the master of the ready economic fix, Mickey pulled out a fistful of twenty-dollar bills and began peeling off several hundred dollars' worth.

"No gracias, senor, porfavor, porfavor, es mi responsibili-dad."

Ethnicity suddenly began trumping economy. Two nearly identical 1947 Chevrolets, lowered to no more than three inches above the mean high-tide mark, oozed into the intersection.

In moments they'd disgorged a squad-sized group of tat-tooed gang members dressed in baggy high-waisted khaki pants, sharp-toed very shiny shoes, oversized buttoned-at-the-neck Pendleton shirts, and knotted nylon stockings pulled over their slicked-back hair.

"No, senor, no senor . . . ," the old man kept repeating as the brown menace began deploying around us in a loose circle. Joe and Freddy positioned themselves on either side of Mickey—and in a move so subtle that none of the constricting ring noticed—Fred slipped his pistol into his right hand, holding it at his side.

Just then another car arrived, and a good-looking young guy jumped out and flashed a sign to the men who'd gathered around us. He had a leader's obvious air of command and authority.

The couple began speaking rapidly in Spanish. He put his hand on the old man's shoulder and listened to him. Then he turned to Mickey.

"Mr. Sanchez says that it was his fault. He rear-ended you, so why're you offering him money?"

Mickey sized him up and smiled.

"Because I'm a nice guy. You got a problem with that? C'mon, lookit his truck. That's a new radiator he's gonna need, new belts, new hoses. Those old Fords got mechanical brakes and stopping's hard with those. Can he afford it? No. Can I? Whaddaya think. See, I grew up round here. He usta bring produce to my mama's store. He don't remember me, but I remember him. Gave me free oranges and apples."

Suddenly the look on the young gang leader's face changed. A broad smile replaced his frown. "Well, Mr. Cohen, that is very nice of you. Very respectful. Please, go ahead, take care of business."

Mickey nodded and stuffed the wad of bills into the chest pocket of the old man's bibbed overalls. His wife touched the crucifix around her neck and mumbled a prayer in Spanish.

"So, you know who I am?" Mickey asked.

"Sure, Mr. Cohen. My name's Marcello. This is White Fence turf now, my turf, my vatos, and I'm the jeffe around here. But a lotta people remember Senor Cohen. And because you are something of a legend I'm inviting you to a little local fiesta—we were headed over there anyways."

Joe looked at Mickey and lifted a diplomatic eyebrow. Mickey nodded back, tapped Fred—whose pistol had already disappeared—and then gestured to Marcello, raising his right hand to chest level like the pope, and nodding his head.

"Like old times, Marcello. Tell your carnales. We'll follow."

Not that we had a choice.

One '47 Chevy was behind us, and the other in front, with Marcello's '50 fastback Chevy with the back end lowered to the deck flanking us. Marcello slid behind the wheel of his car, started it with a loud rap of the pipes, and led our procession off down a nearby side street.

Pulling up in front of a small bright-blue stucco bungalow with a shoulder-high hedge of aloe vera and a little walkway lined with cholla cactus, we could hear the brassy tones of ranchero music coming from a portable record player.

Marcello tapped the youngest kid in the group and whispered to him. Detaching, he went over to Mickey's Brougham and leaned against the front fender with his arms folded. He looked as serious as a Marine sentry manning the gangway of a nuclear sub.

Marcello gestured us into the backyard with a gracious sweep. "I told him to guard your car with his life," he said with a grin.

"They gotta learn young," Mickey said approvingly. I glanced back over my shoulder. Would Mickey make me do that?

Opening the gate, we were suddenly under the drooping branches of a huge pepper tree. A 55-gallon oil drum had been cut in half and turned into an ad hoc industrial-strength grill tended by several women. Two mariachis were strolling around with guitars, and a group of older men were sitting in a half-circle around a very distinguished-looking older man in a very well-worn high-backed leather chair.

"This is my father, Manny," Marcello announced to Mickey as we approached.

Hearing Marcello, the group looked up, suddenly surprised and then apprehensive.

Mickey sized up the situation and extended his hand as the two men's eyes met. Suddenly the group, including Mickey, broke into laughter.

Marcello chuckled. "It's the mota. They thought you were the cops."

I took a closer look. Then the telltale odor hit me. The group was smoking pot.

In short order beers appeared, and then an endless succession of carne asada, carnitas, fajitas, chorizo, steaming beef and chicken tamales, and bowls of fresh salsa, jalapeños, and heaps of freshly cooked tortillas.

After dinner, Marcello's niece, a little girl of eight or nine, did a Mexican folk dance as the assembled group clapped their hands, then, swirling her wide skirt, she bowed to the group's applause.

Sated with spicy food, and a valuable connection made with Marcello, Mickey made a grand exit, stopping to compliment the kid who Marcello had posted to watch the car. He was still leaning against the same fender, in the same position, with his arms folded.

"Ya done good. Not a scratch on her," Mickey said, tucking a twenty-dollar bill in his Pendleton.

Inside the car, Mickey, Fred, and Joe began bemoaning the resultant heartburn. Mickey turned the Brougham around and headed west, back to Brentwood. Exiting the Hollywood Freeway onto Sunset, he belched loudly.

"That's why I hate fuckin' Mexican food. Anybody got some Alka Seltzer?"

11

AUDITIONS

O'DALE IRELAND'S OFFICE was just down the street from the Sunset Grill, on Gardner Street and, coincidentally, right next door to my dad's former laundry.

Office? This dump made low-rent look high. Even the paint used for his name on the door, *O'Dale Ireland, Producer,* looked cut-rate. The waiting room was a symphony of frugal simplicity. Couch: cheap vinyl sagging over crumbling foam rubber; coffee table: cheap avocado-colored Formica over particleboard with a wobbly leg; and capping it all off with a real touch of class was a chipped ceramic ashtray pilfered from Earl Carroll's, complete with genuine cigarette butts.

This was a classic B movie's B-movie production setup. Ireland had obviously gone to great effort to avoid any expense. It couldn't have looked any drearier. Even the two posters facing the couch were tattered and faded.

I found myself thinking twice about sitting on the grimy and probably sticky couch. If I didn't get the part, I'd be stuck with extra dry cleaning.

Fearing it might be a trap, I settled gingerly on the coffee table, counterbalancing to avoid collapsing the bad leg and prematurely emptying the over-full ashtray. Image is important.

On the other side of the thin drywall partition and thinner hollow-core door, I could hear what sounded like an actress speaking lines I recognized from the script.

Listening carefully for what seemed like hours, I detected no gasping, grunting, delighted squealing, or other telltale auditory signs of sexual exertion. A distinct plus. Meant I had some kind of chance.

Finally the door opened. Emerging from Ireland's inner sanctum was one of those young women Hollywood consumed in substantial daily doses. She was a three-B'er: brunette, boobs, butt. As she walked past me at chest-to-eye level, I couldn't help noticing the secondary attributes. It was all above average.

"Thanks for letting me audition, Mr. Ireland. I hope I hear from you soon."

"Call me Dale. And you will."

Ireland wasn't watching the exit. I was; it had been more than twenty-four hours since any of my youthful needs had been met. Or even introduced.

Ireland got right down to business.

"Stevens, I checked your credits, and you're exactly what we're looking for. Our distributor feels that if I sign you, you'll bring a nice level of professionalism to the project, something we don't always get in this kind of film."

"Who's distributing?" I asked.

"Roger Corman's film group. And you'll be working with a couple of old friends, Gary Vinson, who's been over at Warner's, and Judy Nugent."

"Yeah, great. I worked with Judy on the 'Annette' series."

"She seems like a good kid," Ireland offered.

"Great sense of humor, kind of a tomboy, and she has a laugh that would tame a lion. You want me to read?"

He nodded. "Show me what direction you've taken with Cricket."

I closed my eyes for a few seconds, then, tossing the script on his desk, I said, "Okay, this is the scene right after I find out Ashley's character tried to rape my love interest . . ."

Finishing, I turned to find him nodding approval.

"It's yours, Steve, but just so you know, this one's very low-budget, and Johnny's getting most of the money."

"You pay union scale, I play the part. How's that?"

"Scale's yours," he said, offering his hand. "We're going on location in Chillicothe, Missouri. It's about ninety miles north-east of Kansas City. Nice little spot—my hometown, actually. We've got great visuals, and the local high school's providing not only the buildings and the grounds, but the students for our extras."

Missouri? I'd never done a location farther than Iverson's Movie Ranch in Chatsworth, thirty miles from Hollywood. We shook again, and I headed for the door, with that paper-thin carpet feeling like a two-foot layer of marshmallows.

Borrowing Joseph's phone at the Sunset Grill, I called my dad and told him I'd scored a decent role, then dialed John Ashley and thanked him for recommending me for the part.

"Listen, Steve, you're a natural, and having you in that part makes me look that much better. It's hard playing well against bad actors. We'll have a lot of fun with this one, and because the shooting schedule's a little longer, you'll at least make enough dough to afford the rent. Say, are you finally ready to move in? I saw some boxes in the garage."

"How about tomorrow?"

"Drop by and pick up a key."

• • •

Back in my old pad, the phone was ringing as I walked in. Uncle Mickey.

"Say, Kid, what's up? You busy tonight?"

"Nah, just moving my last things from here. I got that part today."

"Great, great. Show up around six. I need you to do me a favor."

I'd picked up a suit from the cleaners, a white shirt and necktie. You never know when you might need to look like a movie star. Suiting up, I headed over to Mickey's and knocked on his door at exactly 1800 hours. Military precision.

Itchy answered. "Come on in, Kid. We just sent out for some Mexican food. Ha-ha."

Joe Sica was talking to an older, very obese man who was puffing on a cigar the size of a baseball bat. Phil Packer was standing behind the bar and gave me a nod. I walked up to the end of the cigar and peered through the cloud of smoke.

"Hi, I'm Steve." I stuck out my hand, guessing where the guy's paw would be under the smoke screen.

"Yeah? How ya doin'?" he said. But no name.

Just then Mickey walked out of his bathroom, trailing an eye-smarting cloud of cologne and drying his hands with a towel.

"Hey, Kid, good to see ya. Come on back here," he said, pointing to the rear bedroom. "I need you to pick up a little guy—gotta big nose and Dumbo ears, name a' Stern—around eight thirty at the airport tonight. He's on"—he looked at a slip of paper—"TWA, flight 226. Okay?"

I nodded.

"So after that, you take him up to the Chateau Marmont on Sunset and Crescent Heights—ya know the place? —and you check with Martin at the desk for the key. This, uh, client's booked into a bungalow. Once he's all in, call this number, as he's gonna want some company, ya know? You wait till the broad gets there, and hang around till she's ready to leave. He ain't gonna take too long, see? But you just keep an eye on things for me, okay? Ya got all that?"

"Sure, Mickey. No problem."

"Then tomorrow, you go get him and bring him here, by nine, okay? He won't be too long here, then you can take him to the airport."

Mickey produced a wad of bills, peeled off three hundreds, and put them in my suit's hankie pocket. "This should cover it, okay? Now, no fuckups. You got that?"

"Uncle Mickey, you don't have to give me anything. I'm happy to do this."

"Kid, you're all right, but take a little advice from ol' Uncle Mickey. Don't ever turn down cash money, huh?"

Three hundred for a few hours' work? Screen Actors Guild scale was $125 a day. This was star money.

Walking back into the living room, I stopped by the bar to mix a rum and Coke. *You just went through another audition,* I told myself. Peeking in the mirror and checking my tie, I poured a hefty shot of Myers's into a splash of Coke. I closed my eyes for a few seconds to get into this new part.

Now it was really showtime.

12

THE OMINOUS STRANGER

STERN, WHOEVER HE was, came off his TWA flight looking exactly as Mickey described him. Big nose, Dumbo ears, dark suit, hat, sunglasses. A little guy, but his bearing was upright, and something about him suggested a kind of menacing strength.

"Mr. Stern? I'm Steve. Mickey sent me."

His chin moved the requisite eighth of an inch. I was getting to know that gesture. It meant: *"Whoever the fuck you are, dirtbag, you don't mean shit to me,"* and without a word he extended his carry-on. It was somewhere between a disrespectful toss and a degrading release. A telling gesture containing the tacit acknowledgment that my status was somewhere slightly below stable lackey, and not quite above slave.

Glancing sideways at him, I realized that my open, youthful countenance, a minor asset in Hollywood, was a deficit that spelled "sap" in whatever world this guy inhabited. But actors are like chameleons, and part of my protective shifting coloration was the ability to become the character the scene called for.

I fished out "respectful assistant," from my bag of film roles, and spent the ten-minute walk to my parked car matching the tempo and heel-strike of Stern's gait, and treating his bag as if it were the president's briefcase containing the nuclear launch codes. By the time we arrived, I had his walk down to close tolerances.

"Backseat, sir?" I asked as I opened my convertible's passenger door. He ignored me and sat in the front passenger seat. Behind the wheel, I quickly changed KFWB Channel 98 Color Radio and the Top-40 AM to a mellow FM station. Maybe music would soothe the whatever-the-hell heebie-jeebie kind of beast Stern was.

When we arrived at the Chateau Marmont, he waited while I came around and opened the door. Removing his bag from the backseat, I matched Stern's steps to the lobby and stopped just ahead of him before the imposing front desk. The man behind gave just a glimmer of acknowledgment, but assiduously avoided making eye contact with either of us. The whole exchange felt creepy. These two had some history.

"Mr. Martin," I began, rolling out my best young-assistant-handling-things-for-the-out-of-town-potentate voice, "I'm picking up a key for one of the garden-side bungalows. Is everything taken care of here?"

"Yes, sir, it is. Follow me, please."

He led us around the courtyard to the bungalow and, inserting the key in the lock, opened the door. "Should you require anything, please just give me a ring."

Stern brushed past us, and Martin handed me the key. I followed him in. He carefully removed his jacket and hat, loosened his tie, removed his shoes, and went to the well-stocked bar. His sunglasses remained in position.

Stern seemed to know where everything was. One hand removed a glass, the other hand grasped a bottle, and lifting the ice bucket's lid, he shoveled in some ice. He still had not spoken a single word.

"May I arrange for some company for you, sir?" I asked. No reply.

"Mr. Cohen's made some special arrangements. She can be here in a few minutes."

He nodded. Taking this for a wholehearted endorsement, I picked up the bedroom's phone, dialed the number Mickey had provided, and listened to the youthful-sounding voice that answered.

"Hi, this is Sherry."

"Hi, Sherry. I'm calling for Mr. Cohen. I'm at the Marmont. Can you please come over?"

"Oh, right. I'll be right there."

I walked out of the bedroom. "Your date's on the way, sir."

He brushed past me into the bedroom and closed the door. The silence in the room was like a thick fog. The whole scenario was so beyond my experience that I forced myself to block the discomfort-bordering-on-panic I was starting to feel.

I sat on a chair by the front door, as far from that closed bedroom door as I could distance myself. I glanced at my watch. Ten fifteen. In ten minutes there was a soft knock.

I don't know what I'd been expecting, but it wasn't what I was seeing.

Sherry was my age, and as softly beautiful as Natalie Wood. Her features were refined and her skin smoothly translucent, all set off by her elegant black cocktail dress. She gave me a sweet smile, and I stood aside as she brushed in. I closed the front door, walked across the living room, and tapped on the bedroom door.

"Enter." The first word he'd spoken to me in two and a half hours.

I squeezed the door handle, not wanting to actually open the door. Stern lay stretched out on the bed on his back in his undershorts, still wearing his sunglasses, with his drink in one hand.

"Your date's here, sir. I'll be waiting in the lobby. Call if you need anything."

Sherry was standing in the middle of the living room. I left the bedroom door ajar, met her eyes for a moment, smiled, and left the bungalow as fast as I could without running.

I found a chair and magazine in the Chateau Marmont's lobby, but it seemed like a cavern. I tried taking some deep breaths, but the compressed tension that had centered in the top of my chest wouldn't release, and I couldn't escape the feeling that I'd allowed myself to become part of something creepily obscene.

I had to get up, take a walk, do something. Stepping outside, it seemed chilly, but the chill I was feeling was more than a drop in the ambient temperature. I cut diagonally across the street, passed Sherry's, another Strip feature, noticing that Joanne Grauer's name was on the marquee.

Joanne was Hollywood Professional School's brilliant, acclaimed jazz pianist. Her first trio album, released a little more than a year before, had received rave reviews. But my brief exposure to Stern had left me feeling creepy and uncomfortable, and I was afraid someone as sensitive as Joanne might guess something was wrong.

I headed for the safe, warm lights of Schwab's Drugstore, which was located just diagonally across the street. Schwab's was a Hollywood fixture, the place Lana Turner, Monroe, and a dozen others had supposedly been "discovered." But even inside, sitting at the soda fountain with a steaming cup of coffee in front of me and a bevy of would-be starlets and wannabe actors fresh from some nearby drama workshop circling around like happy villagers from a musical, the feeling that I'd done something wrong wouldn't leave.

I fished out a Parliament, lit it, and took a deep drag. This was where I belonged, Sunset and Crescent Heights, below Laurel Canyon, on the border of Beverly Hills, looking across at the

SCHWAB'S PHARMACY, A HOLLYWOOD LANDMARK.

arched neon sign of the Garden of Allah, where Hollywood legends indulged in lusts and loves and the only damage done was a press agent's tabloid scandal.

Leaving a tip on the counter, I walked back to the Marmont, Bogie-flipping my smoke into a large potted palm before I stepped into the lobby. Martin, looking like an undertaker, was gesturing for me to take the ringing house phone.

Stern's voice was flat, cold, and hostile. "Get over here."

Christ! He sounds pissed. I half sprinted across the courtyard.

Opening the bungalow's door revealed Sherry—sobbing, half collapsed in a wingback chair, dress torn, lower lip split and bleeding, and her right eye and cheek bruised and swollen. Her upper arms were discolored with finger-shaped bruises where she'd been grabbed.

Stern wasn't visible, but the bedroom door was open. The bathroom's door was ajar. Water was running. Stern's voice hissed out, "Get the bitch outta here."

Kneeling beside Sherry, I helped her to her feet. She was gasping and her body shook convulsively. Taking off my jacket, I draped it over her shoulders and supported her around the waist to get her out of the room.

"You need to see a doctor. There's a hospital not far from here; let me take you."

"No, I don't want to. They'll ask too many questions. Just take me home. I'll take care of it."

I helped her into my car and put up the top. "What the hell happened?"

"He, he . . ." Her breath came in gulps, and she had to push out the words. "He's—one of—he just started beating me."

Her place was only a few blocks away, and when we pulled up she refused my help. Getting out, she left the door open and stumbled toward her apartment. Why should she trust me? I'd called her. I was part of the problem.

Just past Highland Avenue I had to stop to light another cigarette. My hands were trembling too hard to use the cigarette lighter without bracing my elbows against the steering wheel.

What if she changed her mind and called the cops? I'd made all the arrangements. I was as guilty as Stern was.

I sat smoking cigarette after cigarette to calm the waves of nausea that kept surging over me. Just who the fuck was this creep? What kind of perverted sexual pleasure could the bastard get out of doing something like that to such a beautiful girl? She was obviously no pro hooker, probably just a part-time call girl, just a kid, like me, trying to make it in a tough town any way she could.

And knowing this, knowing what he'd done to her, I was

going to have to endure more silent hours of this monster sitting next to me on his way to Mickey's and then to the airport— while I treated him respectfully?

"Christ Almighty," I said aloud, biting the back of my hand. No wonder Mickey had given me three hundred bucks.

It took a long time to make the short drive home.

13

FAMILY HISTORY

EARLY TUESDAY THE phone rang. It was my first morning at the Fountain Lanai, and it took a moment to adjust to new surroundings. I reached across the bed and fumbled with the receiver, finally getting it to my ear on the third ring.

Phil Packer's voice growled, "Kid, scratch pickin' up Stern. Ya hear me? I got it covered. Go back a'sleep."

Sleep?

I sat up and looked at the clock and flopped back down. Six thirty. My spirits rose faster than I did. Damn. Relieved of escort duty. Didn't have to pick up that dirtbag Stern, whoever he was, and endure his hostile silence.

Then I started thinking. *Maybe this guy'd given Mickey a bad report; maybe he hadn't liked the way I'd handled things. Maybe Mickey would—*

Suddenly the apprehension I'd been bottling up spilled over. I wasn't just afraid of a guy like Stern. He'd scare anybody, and that was probably his deal. Hell, he'd chill a zombie's heart.

But I was also afraid of Mickey. I was subconsciously worried he'd be upset that I hadn't pulled off my little pickup–drop-off errand. A three-hour job, for which he'd paid me three days' tax-free acting wages.

Shit.

I climbed out of bed, walking barefoot on the thick carpeting, and opened my bedroom door. Outside, through the sliding glass doors, morning light was filtering through the Lanai's tropical plants and casting slatted shadows on the azure surface of the pool. Lighting a cigarette, I nosed around the apartment like a pup in a new house.

Ashley's bedroom door was ajar, and his bed was still made. Probably had another hot date. No wonder he wanted a roommate. Keep the cobwebs out of the corners.

My list of things to do was sitting where I'd left it the night before:

Tuesday:
Drop off S @ airport.
Call Dad.
Call Hy @ 10:30.

I crossed off the first item and thought about the second.

I showered, shaved, made a cup of coffee, and sat down at the kitchen's bar and dialed. My dad was an early riser, and I knew I'd find him up and catch him before he went to work. He was the manager of the Hollywood Men's Store on Hollywood Boulevard, an upscale menswear shop that catered to people in film and TV by offering a wide range of excellent, well-styled, high-quality—if not custom-tailored—men's clothing.

Dad had been a dancer in vaudeville in his youth, and after we'd moved to Hollywood, he'd worked in film and TV, doing a range of acting roles including a big guest spot on *Mr. District Attorney,* starring David Brian. His managerial position gave him the latitude to do movie work and made him a minor celebrity at the store.

"You're up early," he said. He knew I usually called in the evenings, and probably—as any good parent would—suspected something was up.

"Yeah, well . . ." I hesitated. "Say, I auditioned for a part in a new film. Looks like I got it."

"No kidding!" I could hear the delight in his voice. Dad was always my strongest supporter, and his pride in my career was something that never failed to give me a needed boost when I was down.

"Yeah, you and Mom be home tonight? I'll come by and tell you all about it. I still gotta go by Hy Sieger's and sign the contract."

"Of course. But I'm hearing something else in your voice. A while back you mentioned you'd met that guy Mickey Cohen and gone over to his place. How's that working out?"

How he sensed it, how he knew, I'll never know. But he did, and he knew I knew.

"I've always maintained it takes all kinds of people to make this world, and the more you meet, the more you understand people, the stronger and more perceptive you'll be as a person and an actor. That said, Steve, you know the difference between right and wrong, good and bad; in that I have confidence. I know that guys like Cohen can be pretty interesting, but you need to watch yourself with them. Crowding the line's one thing, but crossing it's another. You watch yourself, okay?"

"Sure, Dad. It's cool; I'm careful. I'll see you tonight. I love you, and give Mom a big hug for me."

Dad had led a hard early life. An orphanage kid, he'd been on the streets of New York's Hell's Kitchen early, earning what he could, honestly—as a tap-dancing street entertainer—and fighting where he had to, viciously.

That much he'd talk about, but there was more of which he never spoke.

• • •

Next on my list was a call to my agent, Hy Sieger.

"Steve, listen, I got Ireland's contract, but I want you to drop by Paramount Studios to see Hoyt Bowers, the casting director. He may have something for you."

After a quick meeting with Bowers—who was always good to me and kept his eye out for a part I could fit—I was feeling better. Walking out at noon, I ran into Jack Gordon, in those days Hollywood's "King of the Extras," who had shared a good deal of my dad's youth and was married to my mother's best childhood friend, Eva.

"Uncle Jack," as I called him, was one of those colorful Hollywood types who'd had more than just a "colorful" past. A big, physically imposing man, Gordon had been a "collector" for the New York mob and—in a quick lateral transfer to avoid some never-disclosed trouble—he'd relocated to the West Coast. In Hollywood, through someone's connection, Jack found a new career where his ability to appear as a convincing heavy created an unending demand for him in a four-decade-long series of extra parts.

"Steve. Whaddaya say; whaddaya know?"

"You have time for lunch, Jack?"

"You askin' *and* buyin'?" Jack chuckled in a *baso profundo* that held all the rich tones of his Bowery past.

"Sure. Lucy's okay?"

"Good by me. Something on your mind, Steve?"

● ● ●

Crossing Melrose Avenue, we walked into Lucy's Café El Adobe. Directly across the street from Paramount's Main Gate, Lucy's offered a great margarita; a tame, pedestrian enchilada; and a healthy serving of Hollywood history.

Jack led us to a dark booth that looked out on the lush plants that lined the patio. Black-and-white studio stills covered the restaurant's walls, some going back to the early years and Hollywood's beginnings. The waitress—in espadrilles, her hair tied back in a red ribbon, and nicely filling out her Mexican peasant dress—patted Jack on the shoulder and left tortilla chips and menus.

"So, it's a coincidence meeting you today. See, I saw your old man at the shop the other day. He's a little concerned about this Cohen guy."

People think of Hollywood and the movie business as a giant industry. In some ways it is, but in other ways it's like working in a small-town department store. Everybody knows everything because everybody knows somebody. And there are no secrets for long.

"Well . . . ," I began, and gave Jack the pitch.

Jack listened thoughtfully, taking a sip of his drink and eating slowly.

"Now, your dad, he'll never talk about this stuff to you because he doesn't want you to get any wrong ideas, but Steve, he loves ya as his son. See, he understands what's going on. He had some rough-edged pals when he was a kid, guys like me; and hell, even guys like Abe Reles—they called him 'Kid Twist.'"

I must have looked blank.

"You never heard of Abe, right? But if I tell you 'Murder, Incorporated'? 'Murder, Ink'?—that make any more uv'a impression?"

Jack pronounced *murder* "moi-da."

"Yeah, sure; I've heard of that. Like a little gang within the Mafia that specialized in taking people out?"

"That's right. See, I knew your pop from way back. When we were young, I was a runner for a bad guy name a' Little Augie Persano, who did a little work for Reles. He had some eyes for your mom—who was such a looker, like Judy Holliday, a little beauty—but she din't care for him and started dating your dad. Well, this Little Augie, one night, he threatens your dad. And your mom, all four feet eleven inches of her, bless her great big little heart, she grabs this baseball bat and beats Little Augie so bad they puts him in the hospital."

"You're kidding me, Jack; my mom did that?"

"Your mom, the pistol. Ya don't wanna cross her. Nah. You shoulda seen it. But this don't sit so good with Little Augie, see, 'cause he can't admit to this, on acount a' he'll be losing some serious face among his boys. So, what's he do, the chickenshit? He tells Reles that your old man done it to him! So, Reles, now he's obligated to help his man—and two of his boys catch your pop coming outta his apartment, and they start working him over. Right there. On the stoop! Jesus, they coulda kilt him—but they just beat him badly, maybe 'cause he's from the old neighborhood they don't bust his head."

"He never told me . . ."

"Nah, why'd he do that? See, he wants ya to respect him, and maybe you'd think he wasn't, what's that word? Courageous? Yeah. But he was."

I absorbed this, but I must have looked doubtful.

"See, because everybody knows, as Reles was the most feared killer in New York, you don't mess wit' him. So, your pop, see, he's a good guy, a nice, intelligent young guy, a guy who reads a lotta books, learns better ways, a guy going up in the world as an entertainer, pretty soon gettin' married. He's too smart to do anything stupid. He and your mom got a little vaudeville bit going, sorta like Burns and Allen. What? He tells Reles it's your mom achully beat the schmuck up, then what's Reles gonna do? Beat up your mom? This guy's crazy that way, and who knows? He mighta. So, no. Your dad does the wise thing. Da manly thing. But he never forgot."

"Well, w-what happened after that?" I stammered. "Was that when we moved?"

"Nah, that's another story. Your pop's debt was paid wit' Abe Reles. But Abe, ha, he gets his later, see. He gets nailed, and cops a plea for talkin' to the grand jury. And da night before he's to testify, he's over in Coney in a hotel, and out da winda he goes. So your pop, understand, later he's playing this big TV part an' he gets even with Abe Reles' ghost."

"Wait, wait . . ." I started laughing. "You mean when my dad played the gangster in that *Playhouse 90* show *Murder, Inc.*?"

"'At's da one. Damn right. Your dad played it beautiful. He's supposed ta push d'udda actor who's playin' Reles out the window, and they rehearse it till they get it down perfectly. They got a mattress outside the winda, and everything. But see, during the performance, which is live to New York and hooked up ta 'kinescope across the country, see, your pop gets caught up in

MEL STEVENS.

the drama. He picks up the Reles character and insteada pushing him out da winda, he picks the guy up and throws him through the goddamn winda past the mattress, right outta sight of the camera!"

I was cracking up.

"And the goddamn director's so pleased with the scene, he don't pay no attention to d'udda actor, who's afraid to say anything 'cause maybe your pop's whacko. So now, your pop's not only got even with Reles' ghost, he got pait for it!"

I was laughing so hard by this time that I could only sputter.

And I knew that tonight, when I saw my dad, I'd assure him that I wasn't heading into a life of crime.

14

FOR A PHOTO OF ANNETTE

DAD ANSWERED MY knock, and I stood for a moment, unable to grasp what I was seeing. His cheek was a livid blue with an angry red welt beginning to form, and there was a contusion over his left eye. Both his lips were swollen, and there was dried blood in the corner of one nostril.

"Jesus, Dad. What'n'hell happened? Did Mom . . ." After my conversation with Jack, I was half fearful he was going to tell me Mom had decked him. She'd been increasingly suffering from what we'd eventually learn was late-onset schizophrenia, and had been periodically withdrawing into a fantasy world of her own, from which she'd emerge in occasional but unpredictable lucid, tearful, or angry outbursts.

"Steve, a couple of pretty tough guys moved in upstairs recently. They've been pushing people here around. All the tenants are frightened of them. They're always throwing loud parties. They turn up the stereo, scream, and jump up and down for hours. I went up to speak to them this afternoon, politely of course, to ask them to keep it down. One of the guys, the biggest one, shoves a pistol in my face, pushes me back against the balcony's rail, and hits me with the barrel a couple of times."

"For Christ's sake, Dad. You didn't call the cops?"

He hung his head, shaking with impotent rage. "He told me, 'Mind your own fucking business, old man.'"

I wanted to hug him, tell him I had the answer, but all I could come up with was "You speak to the manager about them?"

"Speak to him?" Dad put an ice pack to his damaged eye. "They threw him down the stairs and told him if *he* called the cops on them, they'd have their friends take care of him before they were out on bail. And their friends look tougher than they do."

I'd never seen my father so distraught, let alone obviously physically injured. I started for the phone to call the cops. Dad waved me away.

"Steve, guys like this have no consciences. You call the cops, and they'll get bailed out and find you and you'll look like me. That won't do the career any good, and it won't stop them from hurting someone else, maybe one of us."

Above me I could hear the thrum of a big woofer speaker vibrating so loudly the windows shook. Inside, I felt my own rage boiling.

I grabbed the telephone.

"Steve, please, don't call the cops."

"Cops, hell. I'm calling Mickey."

"Cohen? You're calling him, now?"

"Yeah. He's the one the cops called when they couldn't touch some guy that took a poor woman's house down in South Central. One of those screwy legal deals. The law was on the guy's side. He claimed she owed him eight bucks and change for fixing her radio. He filed a lien on her house and foreclosed. He did it all legally, and so the mayor called Mickey on a back line. Mickey sent in his boys, and they took care of the son of a bitch. It was in all the papers."

I dialed Mickey's number. By now I knew it by heart.

Mickey listened. "Okay, Kid, I want you to tell that to Fred. Every detail. Okay?" He put Fred Sica on the line.

I gave him a quick rundown. Fred said, "Uh-huh," a couple of times, then: "Gimme d'address. I'll be right over."

Dad was listening, and when I hung up he gave me a peculiar look. "Get your brother out of here," he said. "I'm putting your mother in the bedroom and locking the door. If something goes wrong, I don't want them in the same place where these guys could find them both. Got it?"

Dad corralled Mom, who was wandering around singing to herself with her mink stole draped over her housecoat.

I nodded and hustled my brother, Reggie, out of his bedroom, where he was doing homework with the radio playing classical music. He was a quiet, studious kid, and I didn't want him to be exposed to what I was beginning to imagine might happen. We gathered up his jacket and books.

Next, I called Jock Putnam, my close friend from HPS, and he agreed to pick Reggie up at the corner and keep him safe until whatever happened happened.

By the time I got back, Fred Sica's car was pulling up to the curb across Hawthorn Avenue. Both Fred and Phil Packer got out, looked over at the apartment building, spotted me, and strolled casually across the street.

• • •

"Dad, this is Fred." Fred offered his hand to my dad, and looked closely at his bruised and cut face.

"Who did this?"

Fred noticed my dad was still trembling and motioned him to sit down at the dining room table.

"All right, Mr. Stevens. You're gonna be okay, see? But I want you to tell me very carefully, so's I unnerstand just what these guys been doin'."

Phil turned a chair around, sat down, and leaned over the back, listening with Fred. When my father finished, Fred looked at him, then at me.

"Okay, I think I got it. Lemme see how I can make this go away. Phil, you want a piece of this?"

Phil lit a cigarette. "Nah. I'm thinking you can handle this one, Fred."

"Yeah, should be okay. I need you, I'll call. Now, Mr. Stevens, you go on, take care of the missus. Phil'll be right here."

Phil smiled as warmly as I'd ever seen him. "If it isn't an inconvenience, you got anything to drink?"

Dad stood up, went to the fridge, and pulled out a bottle of Heineken, which he opened and poured for Phil. Phil put down his cigarette, exhaled a thick cloud of smoke, took a sip, and said in an almost reverential tone, "Now, Mr. Stevens, 'at's one helluva good beer."

Suddenly there was a loud noise as though a door was being torn off its hinges.

Phil looked up and grinned. "Must a' been one of them Hollywood doors you got out here. Usually takes Fred a coupla kicks with the kind we got back home. Y'know, the weather and all. Gotta make 'em a lot tougher."

There was some grunting, a loud smashing noise, and a yell. Phil savored another sip of beer as if it were a fine wine.

"Musta been one of them glass-top tables."

There was a series of increasingly loud thumps. I jumped up. "Jesus, Phil, what's . . ."

"Aw, he's just banging the chump's head against the wall. He hits a stud, like that—it's nice and loud, see. But the plasterboard, it's softer and their heads make a hole and ya gotta do some repairs. Fred likes ta find the studs."

There was a series of hard grunts, followed by audible gasping and coughing.

Phil leaned back, took a drag off his smoke, exhaled, and took a sip of beer. "Damn, Mr. Stevens, that's a good beer. Whatcha call this, anyhow?"

I couldn't hold myself back. "What was all that? What's he doing now?"

Before Phil could answer, there was one huge crash, and a little plaster dust fell on the coffee table in front of the couch where Dad and I were sitting. We looked at each other and then at Phil.

"Kid, you always hear them sounds when Fred's kickin' them in the soft part of their belly, just under the diaphragm. Fred, he use ta fight a little, and he knows all the spots where you work 'em for maximum cooperation."

Heavy footsteps. Then a toilet flushing.

"Now, that's Fred's little head wash. Means he drew a little blood when he punched whomever. So, he puts their head in the toilet, and flushes it. Cleans 'em right up."

This was followed by a bump-bump-bump-bump-bump, and Fred appeared at the front door, dragging the two upstairs occupants by their shirts.

"Mr. Stevens, dese boys came down ta apologize, din't cha, boys?" Fred cracked their heads together. They looked like two of the Three Stooges.

Sica hoisted one of them up, waist high. His face looked much worse than my father's. Both eyes were swelling shut, his lips were cut and puffy, and one tooth was missing and the bloody stump of another was drooling clots of blood and threads of spittle.

"Honest, Mr. Stevens, we're really sorry," he slobbered. "We didn't know you was family to Mr. Cohen. We didn't . . ."

Fred gave him a short knee to his ribs and hoisted his partner up. "Now, you. You got sumthin' to say, shitbag?"

"Yeah, yeah, I'm sorry, man, sorry. We didn't know . . ."

My dad was trying to control his anger, and I could see his

fists clenching and unclenching and the vein on the side of his unbruised temple standing out.

"Shitheads like you never know until it's too late. And it's too late. Fuck you both. And don't let me, or anyone in this

Autographed photos of Annette Funicello proved to be very popular with Mickey's pals.

building, ever see your faces again or hear your goddamn noise."

Fred dragged them out onto the steps and kicked them both soundly in the ass. One fell down into the flower bed, and the other crawled down the remaining steps.

"So, problem taken care of, Mr. Stevens. They'll be moving soon. You have a good evening now." Fred was pulling off a pair of black leather gloves with thick ridges running across the backs. Sap gloves. I hadn't noticed them before.

"And say, Steve, if it wouldn't be too much trouble, could you get me one of them autograph pictures of Annette for my pal's kid? Her name's Annette, too."

"I'll get it next week," I said, not knowing just how to rightfully thank them. *Nice work, guys. Excellent example of conspiracy to commit felony breaking-and-entering, assault and battery with intent to commit great bodily harm, as well as maiming, mayhem, disfiguring, and extensive property damage.*

Fred and Phil stood up, waved as though they were just leaving from a short social visit, and left.

Dad looked at me and shook his head from side to side. "Mickey's boys?"

"Uh-huh," I managed.

"You see what they did?"

How could I not have? "Yes," I said.

"So now you know for sure?"

"Yes."

"You ever seen anything like that before?"

"No."

"They can do that to anyone, even you, if you get on their wrong side."

"Yes."

"You be very careful. Very careful. Now, go get your brother."

I could tell he wanted to be alone, comfort my mother and

my brother when he returned. I called Jock and told him to meet me.

It was after dark when I finally pulled into the underground parking garage at the Lanai. I'd forgotten to tell my father about the audition and the part.

The phone was ringing when I opened the door. It was my dad.

"You were in such a hurry to get out of here, you forgot to tell me all about the new film."

"Okay, Dad," I said, relieved to be discussing something as far away from the evening's grim reality as a movie.

"Fade in on a classic little Midwestern town . . . A new Caddy's pulling out of the driveway of a nice-looking house on a tree-shaded street . . ."

15

SAY IT WITH FLOWERS

"Look, Steve, you take it or leave it. I got four more smaller parts from Fox, Universal, RKO, and Paramount. They all require some driving, but the farthest location's about ninety miles. The Paramount job's local and probably going to give you about week's work."

Hoyt Bowers's job didn't work out; even thought I'd walked in wearing my uniform, the director didn't think I looked like a Marine. I wish Uncle Sam had agreed. But I did pick up a couple of days on *Perry Mason.*

My career as a working actor had been enjoying a period of relative consistency. Hollywood works that way for the average actor. You're either deluged with work or worrying about getting enough to pay next month's bills. Even big-name stars experience the same employment fluctuations. The major difference was that they measured their paychecks in six and even seven figures.

The last few weeks had been solid work. I'd finish one shoot and run to another, and I needed a day or two to get ready for a cast meeting on *High School Caesar*. It looked as though I'd be working right up until we left for Missouri, and I had to take care of a number of obligations before I left.

I wanted to get the signed picture of Annette I'd promised to Phil Packer, for what he and Fred had done to help my dad. And it gave me an excuse to call Mickey. I hadn't spoken with him since that afternoon, and I felt remiss in not having kept in closer touch.

I picked up the phone and called. Phil Packer answered.

"Hey, Phil. I have that photo for your pal's daughter."

"Great, Kid, bring it by anytime. Where ya been? How'd you hear about Mickey?"

"Hear? Is something wrong?"

"Well, we had to take him to the hospital last night. He was having bad stomach pains."

"Where'd you take him?"

"West L.A. place called Midway Hospital; you know it?"

"Sure. The Jewish hospital, down on Pico?"

"'At's the one."

"What'd the doctor say?"

"Thought it was bleeding ulcers. They're gonna keep him for a few days, make sure he's okay."

Ulcers? It didn't surprise me. Mickey was obviously a guy who lived in a world of stress. His was a business that seemed to consist of running hundreds of other businesses—all illegal, all carrying the penalty of arrest, indictment, court battles, prison, and even possible execution.

And many of the people I'd become aware of, while they might be cunning, practical, and skilled at crime, were people who took chances and lived lives where violence, danger, anger, and fear were served up in copious daily doses.

Not a business where you found a lot of contemplative Cistercian monks leading lives of spiritual discovery.

"Can he have visitors?"

"Yeah, sure. Freddy's already down there. We'll be going down pretty soon."

I hung up and thought about an appropriate gift. With an ulcer, Mickey probably couldn't eat any candy, and he never drank. He chewed on cigars, but it seemed unlikely they'd condone even that in the hospital. I could probably find a nice bathrobe at my dad's store. Nope. That wouldn't work. He had closets full of monogrammed silk bathrobes. That left flowers.

Flowers for Mickey? Yeah, of course. Why not. But what kind?

• • •

I headed down to Parisian's Flowers on Sunset and Gardner, right across from the Sunset Grill. I waved at Joseph as I pulled up. Mrs. Parisian was spraying down the buckets of cut flowers that sat under the striped awning in front of the shop.

"Steve Stevens. Where have you been? The only time we ever see you anymore is at the movies or on TV."

"Mrs. P., I'm on a mission of mercy. A pal's in the hospital, and I need to take him a really nice spray of flowers. What kind should I pick?"

"Well, dear, as I've told you before, flowers are a language. Different blooms play different tunes. And different hues will lift the blues. How ill is your friend, and how much do you want to spend?"

"Whatever you suggest, Mrs. P. And price? You always give me a nice price. So whatever . . ."

Just then the phone rang, and Mrs. Parisian signaled me to wait for her to take the call. I nodded okay and began looking around the shop.

In the back, behind the frosted-glass doors of one of the big coolers—where they kept the flowers at a constant thirty-eight degrees—was an enormous wreath at least four feet in diameter that had been designed around a field of dark greens with a center of white hydrangeas. Into this were skillfully woven dozens of irises, roses, gardenias, and lilies. Placed across the display's crown was a six-inch black velvet ribbon with the words "Rest in Peace" beautifully inscribed in Gothic letters.

Mrs. Parisian joined me. "It's lovely, isn't it? We made it for a funeral day before yesterday, but they never came to pick it up. It took us hours."

I stared at it for a few seconds longer, and then an idea popped into my head. I turned to Mrs. Parisian.

"What's something like that cost?"

"Why, they paid over eighty dollars. And because it's so large, it includes an easel as well, so it can stand up."

"And they never picked it up?"

"No, they never did. We'll just have to throw it out."

"What would you charge me for it? My pal's got a good sense of humor."

Mrs. Parisian tilted her chin and put a finger to her lips. "If your friend's very ill, then the humor would be a trifle questionable, wouldn't it?"

"Ulcers?"

"Ulcers? Well, probably not fatal, is it. Perhaps . . ."

"He likes a good laugh, and maybe, since it's sort of Charles Addams, maybe it would cheer him up?"

"Well, Steve, you'd know that better than I would, but perhaps it might."

"So, how much?"

"Three dollars. For the easel."

"Deal of the week, Mrs. P. I'll take it."

Mrs. Parisian wrapped the wreath in clear cellophane while I put my car's top down, and together we put it in back with the easel. In twenty minutes I was walking through the doors of the sedate Midway Hospital.

Spotting the nurses' station on the fourth floor, I approached, thinking I'd ask if one of them would take it to Mickey. The three on-duty RNs took one look at the wreath, the wooden easel, and me, and simultaneously shook their heads in severe disapproval.

"Young man," said the eldest of the three, looking down her nose at me, "your sad attempt at humor is superseded only by your lack of sensitivity to someone with a very serious medical condition. If you insist on taking that abysmal funereal floral display into Mr. Cohen's room, while he may consider you a friend, I'd personally and very seriously question the nature of your relationship."

"Did you memorize that?" I deadpanned. "That was wonderful. Excellent delivery. Terrific. You sounded just like Joan Crawford."

"Stick around here any longer, buster, and you're going to look like Willie the Worm. He's down there. Go."

Taking a bow, I began toting my wreath down the shiny, waxed floor toward the two men standing guard at the door. Freddy Sica took one look at the enormous wreath and started chuckling.

"Je-zus H. Kee-rist, Kid. What's this?"

"Would you take it in to him?" I asked.

"You nuts?"

I was beginning to have grave doubts about my graveside humor. But I was on a roll.

"How about this guy?" I indicated the cast-iron locomotive boiler standing next to him with a blank look on his face. I looked again. I must have been wrong. There were no rivets.

"This here's Sid. He don't get it."

I looked around to see just what it was Sid wasn't getting.

Fred pointed at the ribbon and turned his palm up. "He don't read."

"Silly me," I quipped. "I might have guessed. I could read it for him."

Sid looked like a refugee from TV wrestling. All he needed

was a black hood and tights. The hood to cover the cauliflower ears—and everything else.

"Listen, Kid, you wanna take it in, okay. But you take it. We don't want nuthin' to do with it."

Knocking on the door, I heard Mickey's muffled voice saying to come in. Squeezing sideways, I humped the big wreath in and set it on the easel on the floor just to the right of his bed.

Mickey put down the magazine he was looking at and broke up.

"Where'n'hell did you get that? Steal it off someone's grave?"

"Uncle Mickey, you don't miss a trick," I lied. "Bagged it over at the Hollywood Cemetery. Took it right off some big-shot studio banker's grave. Figured he won't miss it."

"Ha-ha-ha. You're okay, Kid. You got balls. I can hear it now, 'EXTRA, EXTRA! Read all about it, flowers missing from Big Shot's grave!'

"Say, that's so good you can put it outside. Maybe then the whole fuckin' world will leave me alone."

16

MICKEY TAKES A BITE OUT OF CANDY BARR

"**S**O, KID, CAN ya get us a nice table tonight at Earl Carroll's?" Mickey was asking.

Mickey had come to rely on some of my connections by now, and I didn't want to disappoint him. Still, Earl Carroll's was one of Hollywood's classiest clubs, a sparkling gem in the crown of Hollywood nightspots. You couldn't get into the place unless you knew somebody or, better yet, were somebody.

"Sure," I said casually, not having a clue if I could or not. "Meet you there at eight."

Sunset Boulevard was awash in giant searchlights. Limousines swooshed up to waiting footmen, discharged their cargo of sparkling stars, and evaporated.

Being a semi-somebody who knew a few actual somebodys usually worked, but that damn bouncer from the Sea Witch was outside, in a tux that looked like he'd pulled it over his football uniform.

And it was obvious he remembered me. From the smirk on his face, I guessed that despite all my charm on the previous occasion, Bozo was still underwhelmed.

EARL CARROLL'S.

"You again?" Bozo's headshake was one of those wide-spec nonverbal gestures that implied disdain, amazement at my effrontery, and absolute intransigence. Quite a repertoire.

I tried a wink. Nope. His attitude hadn't changed.

Mine, however, had. "I need a table for five," I said, my thumbs halfway up my sternum, pinkies out, just like Mickey. "And I want a booth in the back."

"We're full up, chump. Beat it."

This guy's resistance to charm was amazing.

I moved in close, slid one extended pinkie under his lapel, and rotated my thumb so it pointed over my shoulder. He looked down on me from his lofty height like he was going to squash me.

"Bozo, a guy with talent like yours could go places. First, though, we gotta do something about your earwax buildup. Table for five. Pronto."

My attention-adjustment gesture had worked. Bozo's pit-bull eyes were now focused on Itchy, Freddy, and Joe Sica strolling up the red carpet behind me, surrounding a grinning Mickey.

Bozo was responding to his training program. If I wasn't yet a face in his midget-brain Rolodex, Mickey was.

"Yeah, yeah, well, like I said, no problem. Fix ya right up."

Flush with my newly projected power, I rocked back on my left heel, slipped my thumbs into my waistband, and did a Cagney pants-pull.

"That table's coming right up, Uncle Mickey."

"Nice job, Kid," Mickey said approvingly. I caught Itchy nodding to Freddy. I did a credible Cagney.

Bozo did a quick recon with the maître d' and they both came forward, doing everything but bowing and scraping as they ushered us in. Mickey passed out several Hamiltons.

I was no stranger to celebrity, but Hollywood can amaze even its own best cynics. Earl Carroll's looked like a casting call for a C. B. DeMille epic. Everybody in filmland was here.

On stage, Louie Prima and Keely Smith were into the first bars of "Embrace Me," and as we walked past the bandstand, Louie pointed his finger at Mickey. Mickey blew him a kiss. Out of the corner of my eye I saw Hedda Hopper note the gesture.

We angled toward the table, intersecting the trajectory of a waiter wheeling a magnum of Mumm's in a silver bucket.

"Mr. Sinatra wanted you to have this, sir . . ."

Mickey looked up, scanning the elevated dais across the dance floor. Seeing Sinatra, he touched his right index finger to his eyebrow, tossing a little "Oh, yeah" chin-lift in Frank's direction.

My attention suddenly focused on Itchy, who had started scratching his trigger finger. I'd seen him do that before, with serious results. It was a gesture that a bad scriptwriter would have labeled as "fraught with meaning . . ."

"Aw, shit, Steve, DUCK!"

Every former Marine will resonate to that single most important four-letter word in the Corp's boot-camp survival vocabulary. He'd gotten to "du" and I was down.

Around me, all these black-gabardined knees were bouncing. Above me, no sounds of incoming rounds. Instead, it sounded like a laugh track from *I Love Lucy*.

I'd been had.

"Jeezuz Ke-rist, Kid, what the hell ya doin' under there?" Mickey could hardly get the words out.

I emerged from my impromptu duck-'n'-cover drill to see Itchy with tears rolling down his cheeks.

"What the fu—" I couldn't complete the sentence.

Even the normally taciturn Sica was grinning.

"Glad you could put in an appearance," Itchy quipped and slapped me between the shoulder blades.

"Some reflexes, huh?" Freddy chortled.

Just then the waiter popped the cork. I involuntarily twitched, and this brought another round of guffaws from the boys. The waiter placed the first glass before Mickey, who solicitously handed it to me.

"Kid, you're all right. Ya know when to duck. 'S'important. I ain't alive this long cuz I'm some tough guy, right? Nah. Five times they tried killin' me, right? And I'm alive cuz I ducked."

"He even ducked a shotgun outside a' Sherry's," Freddy added.

Apparently "duck" was as important a verb in Mickey's lexicon as it had been for me at the U.S. Marine Corps Recruit Depot. Everybody lifted glasses as Mickey uttered the ultimate word of wisdom.

"It croaked poor Neddy Herbert," Itchy confirmed.

Mickey tapped my hand. "Them guys was mad-dog punks, using a shotgun like that. It ain't human."

Apparently there was a strict protocol about the weapons used for mass assassination, and in Mickey's book, "inhuman" shotguns were excluded. Maybe a Thompson submachine gun would be okay?

Onstage, Prima and Smith were bantering back and forth between numbers. Prima lifted his hand to get the crowd's attention, picked up the mike, and moved so that he was facing Mickey.

"Ladies and gentlemen," Prima said with reverence, "this number is for my good pal Mickey over here, enjoying the show. We call him the "King of Sunset Strip.""

Prima turned and counted a downbeat, and the band started playing. Frank Sinatra and two or three of his party were approaching from the right side of the room. Just then Bobby Darin and a woman were walking up the three steps from the dance floor on the left.

Their combined body-Italian was an easy read. This was no mutual-admiration society. The two singers stopped with exactly seven feet between them. I made a quick mental note. Itchy had explained that this was the distance where most gunfights take place.

Mickey picked up on the vibe and played it like a violin. Not only was he the King of Sunset Strip, he was the mediator as well.

"Frank, c'mon now, shake hands with this kid, huh? Hey, don't we all gotta make way for the next generation?"

Sinatra stared across the two-and-a-third yards as though it were the Grand Canyon. Darin—his junior in every way—stepped across the chasm and extended his hand.

"Mr. Sinatra, you're still the king."

Sinatra, always the alpha dog in the showbiz pack, suffered through the formalities and acknowledged the younger man's gesture. Darin turned to Mickey and offered his hand. Mickey clasped it, covering it with his left. Darin was dismissed.

As Darin left, Sinatra's face relaxed. "Mickey, I just wanted to say thanks for everything."

Mickey, basking in magnanimity, shook his head. "Frank, don't mention it. What're friends for, huh?"

"Sure, Mickey, but you were there when some of those friends wouldn't even return my calls."

A lopsided little guy with a big Speed Graphic press camera, pockets bulging with the four-by-five-inch plates those cumbersome antiques digested, touched Sinatra on the arm.

"Mr. Sina—"

Sinatra recoiled as if the man's fingers were a snake.

"Get the fuck outta here, shithead! Beat it!"

The little man's face contorted as if he'd been slugged.

Mickey held up his hand.

"Frank, Frank, easy now. Remember the last time you punched someone in this joint. There was a lot of bad publicity then, remember?"

"Yeah, Mickey, you're right, like always."

Sinatra's narrow-shouldered shrug said it all. He'd garnered more than his share of negative publicity for his volatile temper. The affable, relaxed casual persona he projected onstage belied his belligerent, uptight offstage behavior.

Sinatra shook Mickey's hand again. "Listen, call me next week, okay?"

Mickey watched him as he made his way through an adoring crowd.

"Bullfighters. Goddamn bullfighters."

I must have looked puzzled. Cohen poked me with his knuckle.

"See, Kid, broads always go for bullfighters. Ava Gardner with Frank, and that bitch Virginia Hill with Benny Siegel. Both of 'em went for bullfighters."

"Yeah," Itchy interjected, "but Bugsy took a slug for that broad. Remember?"

"An' Frank stuck his head in an oven for Ava."

"Awph," Mickey puffed. "Somebody gonna die cuz some broad's bangin' a bullfighter? It ain't gonna be me."

"You could send her a package, right?" Itchy stage-whispered. I didn't know what it meant, but it got a chuckle.

Mickey abruptly gestured to Freddy that he was ready to leave. Freddy stood up. Joe Sica got up on his side. Itchy dropped some bills on the table. Mickey and I slid out of the booth, and we all made our way past Prima, who was holding court at a table near the bandstand.

"Great opening, Louie," Mickey said, patting Prima's shoulder as we walked past. The famous singer half stood, but Mickey gestured for him to remain seated.

• • •

Twenty minutes later we pulled up at the Largo, a burlesque house that featured strippers.

Joey D. was waiting as if he'd been cued, and he escorted us inside. This was no Crescendo. The walls were painted flat black, and the low ceiling was hung with stage lights. It had "joint" written all over it.

Joey D. had a big booth in back that overlooked the room. It was obvious that this was Mickey's special spot, as a "RESERVED" sign was whisked off and Joey D. bowed us in.

On the stage a lissome brunette was finishing a feather dance to the last bars of a scratchy recording of Beethoven's Moonlight Sonata. As she stepped down, Joey D. waved her over to the booth.

"Mickey, this here's Amy Archerd."

Mickey, tapping his reservoir of elegant charm, kissed her hand. The gesture was so bizarre that my mouth must have dropped open. Freddy flipped my mandible into locked position.

Amy, still modestly clad in her G-string and pasties, slid in next to me. I was no stranger to the female form, but I didn't usually get this close to a naked woman before the first date. Here I was, biceps-to-boob with a woman who was causing an escalating range of penile responses.

What passed for a band had mustered, and they began to play their version of Frankie Avalon's "Venus." Largo's fat emcee gave a couple of hubba-hubbas, and the drummer did a rim-shot. "And now our lady of the evening, Miss Candy Barr!"

A pin-spot followed a stunning, voluptuous blonde as she undulated across the stage, throwing every inch of her nuts-numbing body into the process.

A guy a table away looked like he was having a stroke.

"Joey, that's some kinda lady."

She began shedding the disposable elements of her costume. With each piece, more gorgeous skin was exposed, and everyone in the booth, Amy included, was watching the performance.

"Mickey," Joey D. said, "that's the broad I been tellin' ya about."

Itchy swallowed audibly. Candy Barr was standing on the runway, bathed in a soft spot, peeling off the last of the least, and flexing and rippling every muscle in her body.

Sica gave a low whistle.

"Now, she's got class, Joey!" Mickey whispered, rising to his feet as she finished her number. He was clapping with his hands over his head.

Noticing nobody else in the club had risen, Mickey cleared his throat loudly and motioned to the patrons around us to stand.

"On yer feet, ya bums!" Mickey shouted. "Whadda you, a buncha chumps? Give the lady a big hand."

It was as though the applause-track had been turned on.

From the runway, Candy was taking all this in. She blew Mickey a kiss. He enthusiastically gestured for her to join our party.

Joey D. went over to help her down and escort her to the booth.

Mickey, still standing, motioned me to move over. I was developing a visible relationship with Miss Amy.

"Have a seat, Miss Barr, I'm . . ."

"I know who you are." She reached over and pinched Mickey's plump cheek. "You're Mickey Cohen the gangster!"

"Nah, I'm Mickey Cohen the businessman."

"Too bad then, 'cause gangsters are sexy." Candy Barr was no Campfire Girl.

Mickey's eyes popped out.

"Sexy? How's that?"

"Well, they take what they want, don't they?" Candy emphasized what any man would want with a shake that sent her pastie tassels into a frenzy.

Candy slipped in beside me. Seeing my tumescently obvious state of visible happiness at being sandwiched between two all-but-naked beauties, she winked. "Hi ya, sweetie. You're cute. But you gotta be careful. Don't let that thing out. It could getcha in trouble."

Let it out? Now it was my turn for cardiac capers. This was one hell of a lot of woman, and I could feel her performance-warmed arm and breast against the sleeve of my tux. I'd never been short of male hormones, and tonight I was producing enough testosterone to make a major deposit in the Federal Sperm Bank.

My eyes all but rolled back in my head. It didn't get any better than this. I was surrounded by two of the most beautiful naked women I'd ever seen. And there was no exit.

"Well, doll, the DA'd agree wit ya. So what can I say, I ain't shy."

Candy gave a little giggle that turned into a wiggle and set the tassels dancing. I wasn't the only guy in the booth that had to squirm to relieve pressure in the groin area.

"So, tell me"—Mickey dropped his voice to a more intimate tone—"how d'ya feel about bullfighters?"

"Bullfighters?" Candy cocked her head to one side. "Aw, they look like little fags in sequined knickers."

Mickey's smile grew until his eyes crinkled shut. It didn't take a psychic to read that expression.

Uncle Mickey had found his dream girl.

17

PRELUDE TO A HIT

"**K**ID, IT'S UNCLE Mickey. Listen, we're meeting at Rondelli's out on Ventura Boulevard in Sherman Oaks tonight. Now, you remember that stripper Amy Archerd we met at the Largo the other night?" I want you to pick her up and bring her out there, ya got it?"

Like I could forget her? Her name was a spoof, parodying the well-known *Daily Variety* columnist, Army Archard. Her body could provide a year's worth of wet dreams to the nation's Boy Scouts.

"Sure, Uncle Mickey. Rondelli's. What time?"

"Okay, make it around ten thirty. Take her number down. She'll tell you where to meet her."

• • •

I wasted about six-tenths of a nanosecond calling her.

"Sure, I remember you, Steve," she purred. "But my car's in the shop, and I'll have to go home and change. So why don't you just pick me up at the Largo at eight thirty? I don't live too far away, just over on King's Road off Sunset."

It seemed as though that might be cutting it close, given Friday traffic, and I was about to suggest having her take a taxi, but the little shoulder devil popped up: *What? You're complaining about getting to spend a little extra time with a broad like that? Gimme a break!*

That little shoulder devil seemed to be making a lot of suggestions lately, but I was as obsessive about time and being prompt as Mickey was about washing his hands. I hated being late, and I prided myself on being to-the-minute punctual. Fearing that something unforeseen might happen, I'd often arrive as much as an hour early for an appointment.

My brain did a compulsive but lightning-swift *Stevens Precision Unforeseen Contingency Timeline* calculation based on a 120-minute projection:

- RENDEZVOUS W/AMY @ CLUB LARGO: 2230 hrs.
- Allow 10 minutes TIME-IN-TRANSIT to King's Road location.
- Allow minimum 45 minutes "change" time.
- Allow 20 minutes for unspecified female memory lapses, e.g., "Where did I leave my . . ."
                    CUMULATIVE TIME: 75 MINUTES
- Proceed in a northwesterly direction over Laurel Canyon
- Estimated T-I-T: 25 minutes.
                    CUMULATIVE TIME: 100 MINUTES
- Proceed to Rondelli's with contingency 15 minutes per parking, lipstick application, makeup/hair adjustments, etc.
                    TOTAL TIME: 115 MINUTES
        CONTINGENCY FOR MURPHY FACTOR: 05 MINUTES

It was just shaving it way too close for my comfort. And that was based on driving over Laurel Canyon, which I was less than partial to taking at night.

Pulling up in front of the Largo, I could see Amy standing and chatting with one of the red-jackets. She waved, and he jumped a few steps ahead of her to open the door. Precisely ten minutes later we pulled up in front of a nice fourplex.

"Come on in. I'll make it as fast as I can," she said.

"I can wait."

"No, I insist, please," she said.

I might have resisted, but she *had* insisted. And she was just too beautiful to be resisted.

"Honest, I'll just be a second," she said, opening the door. "You just sit down on the couch, I'll pour you a nice glass of wine, and you can relax."

Yeah, right. I was already looking at my watch. And so was everybody else in the damned apartment. On all the living room walls were kitschy framed prints of children with huge eyes, by a popular artist of the time named Keane.

Wineglass in hand, I plunked down on the pink vinyl couch. That lasted about thirty seconds before I got the time-twitches. *Damn, I hate being caught short on time. Shit.*

I heard a door close, and water running.

Great. She's in the shower. That was pretty fast.

I put the wineglass on the coffee table, stood up, and looked at my watch, trying to estimate just how long she'd take. And began pacing.

I'd done about three circuits of the room when I heard the shower go off, and I chanced to look up. A full-length mirror in her bedroom was clearly visible from where I was standing. And so was she, coming into her bedroom with only a towel. With which she immediately began drying herself.

I stopped pacing. I forgot about my watch. It was impossible to do otherwise. She was perfect. There were no pasties or G-string. Just Amy. Long legs, beautifully rounded thighs and hips, towel patting her breasts, she turned and bent over to open a drawer.

I sucked in a lungful of air and couldn't release it. All thoughts of Mickey, of time, stopped.

Frozen, my overwhelming reactions enveloped me. Mind ceased functioning. Breath came quickly. Sensations of warmth-becoming-hot emanated from my groin.

Her back still to me, she took a white garter belt, panties, and some stockings from the drawer, stepped into the garter belt, smoothed the straps down each leg, placed her foot on the nightstand next to the bed, leaned forward, and began rolling one stocking up her leg.

Her panties were still on the chest of drawers.

It was a Fredrick's of Hollywood moment.

Securing each stocking on her thighs, she straightened, put each foot into her spike-heeled shoes, and turned—catching me staring at her in her mirror. She tilted her head, as if making a quick decision, and then, lifting her right index finger—motioned.

I had no sensation of crossing the living room, or passing through her bedroom's doorway. It was as though I'd glided, led by my now-more-than-obvious erection. I reached her and both her hands touched my cheeks, caressed my neck, touched my shoulders, and held for a moment while she kissed me.

Her lips seemed to draw the breath out of me, and with her mouth still on mine, her palms exerted gentle pressure and I found myself seated on her bed, and her hands undoing my belt and zipper. She knelt over me and guided me into her.

If her touch and image had suggested sexual fantasies before at the Largo and afterward, now the fantasies were being met with a reality that was so intense it would have burned the pages of those plain-brown-wrapper books you could order by mail, and the common black-and-white pictures of sex that occasionally showed up in barracks and dormitories.

I was no virgin, but at nineteen my sexual experience was limited. Hers, however, was not. It was simultaneously passionate and subtly tender. And it opened a door I had never known—or even suspected—to exist.

With her undulating compressing rhythm, my breath came more quickly. I began losing focus, until only the huge eyes of children in those prints were clear.

And then the wave broke, collapsed.

And after, the surge receded, and the beach was left damp.

• • •

"Have we taken too long?" she whispered, dismounting me. I struggled to sit up, but my stomach muscles wouldn't support the effort. I had to roll on my side and prop myself up with one weak arm.

I blinked, trying to make my watch's face visible.

"Oh, shit," I said, staggering and trying to hike up my pants. "We gotta get going. Uncle Mickey wanted us there at ten thirty."

Still wearing only the garter belt, stockings, and spike heels, she helped me to my feet, took a dress from her closet, slipped into the bathroom for a moment, and while I was still trying to regain my balance, she appeared, fully dressed.

At King's Road and Sunset, we were five minutes from Laurel Canyon, but when we arrived at its juncture on Sunset, it was obvious that traffic was at an impasse. Solid—both ways. It made no sense. How could it be blocked both ways?

I stayed on Sunset three more blocks to Ogden, turned left and then right on Franklin, which ran parallel to Sunset.

Gunning the Pontiac's powerful 400 cubic-inch V-8, I roared down Franklin toward Highland and the Cahuenga Pass, but even there we were bucking a heavy stream of Hollywood Bowl traffic. I took a sidestep shortcut east then, with the light at Highland Avenue, cut across and down past Barham to Ventura Boulevard in Studio City.

We were now about three miles from Rondelli's, but even

here the traffic was almost solidly bumper-to-bumper. It took us twenty more minutes just to reach Laurel Canyon.

It was now well after eleven.

At Coldwater Canyon, police cars with flashing red lights had blocked two of Ventura's four lanes. Traffic officers in reflective vests and white gloves were directing traffic down side streets. Behind us, two unmarked black Ford sedans with magnetized gumballs slapped on their roofs sped by and turned into what appeared to be Rondelli's.

Amy's eyes widened, and her hand touched my arm.

"Isn't that Rondelli's?"

"Looks like something bad's happened," I managed to croak out, wondering if it had been Mickey or one of the Sicas, Joey D., Itchy, or Phil.

I turned on the radio, but the midnight newscast had no local news, and we drove in near-silence all the way down to Sepulveda, crossed back over into Beverly Hills, and then along Sunset to Kings Road. It took over an hour.

"Steve, I really don't want to be alone tonight. Will you please stay?"

I shook my head. My emotions were so conflicted—torn between my strong and increasing attraction to her, and my irrational obligation to Mickey—that I could do nothing but shake my head again.

"I dunno, Amy. I gotta get back to my place, see if anybody's called. I'm really worried."

Confused, uncertain, fearful would have been more accurate, but I couldn't even articulate those emotions. She slid across the front seat to kiss me, and as she got out of the car her dress pulled up over her thighs and the white-ribbon straps and icing of the garter belt's lace.

I pulled a hard U-turn, chirping rubber as the Pontiac's hydro shifted, and didn't take my foot off the accelerator until I'd reached the Fountain Lanai.

18

ZERO-DARK-THIRTY PHONE CALLS

As usual, John Ashley wasn't home when I tiptoed in around 2:00 a.m.

There was a bottle of Bacardi 151-proof rum sitting on the kitchen's bar. I found a can of Coke, a glass, filled it with ice from the fridge, and made myself a stiff drink. I took a long pull and, noting the drainage, refilled and walked into the living room

Collapsing on the couch in the dark, I lit a final cigarette and sat looking out at the pool, trying to sort out the little information I had. The radio reports were still sketchy. They hadn't identified the victim or victims of what they were referring to as an "apparent shooting homicide at a prominent Valley nightspot."

Apparent? What was apparent about a shooting victim lying dead on the floor in a restaurant?

So I knew someone was dead, and I knew I'd been told to get there at ten thirty. And Mickey'd wanted me there, with a stripper he'd met only a few nights before. Why?

I knew Mickey was Hollywood's A-list gangster. Maybe I didn't feel comfortable admitting I knew, or that I had chosen to keep ignoring the fact, but that's what he was.

My little shoulder angel piped up: *It doesn't matter what you know, or why, or how. Your guardian angel just saved you.*

I'd been late getting to Rondelli's in part because my short-cut, Laurel Canyon—the narrow, tree-lined, twisting two-lane road connecting Sunset Boulevard in Hollywood across the eastern spur of the Santa Monica Mountains into Sherman Oaks and Ventura Boulevard—had been traffic-choked both ways. Going east to Highland and over the Cahuenga Pass, I ran into another traffic jam. Now I knew why. The cops had blocked off Ventura.

To have made it exactly on time, had there been no traffic, I'd have had to have left Amy's earlier—as planned. Leaving when we did, had I not encountered the traffic, I'd have been perhaps an hour late. I'd always known sex was a good thing; now I was firmly convinced.

Luck 'n' timing, and a coincidental combination of estrogen, testosterone, and cops blocking Ventura. Maybe I didn't yet know what I'd missed, but whatever it was, my lack of attendance was obviously a plus. I finished my drink, poured another, and felt the rum wash over me.

I opened the sliding door, took a deep breath of cool night air, crushed my Parliament out in the large banana-tree planter outside, flopped into bed, and fell asleep.

• • •

Until the phone rang.

"Steve, you awake?"

I glanced at the radio clock. "Awake? Jesus, Craig, man; it's, like, three thirty."

"I've been calling since seventeen hundred. Where've you been."

"Shit, you wouldn't believe me if I told you. Let me go back . . ."

"No way; wake your jarhead ass up. We have to talk."

"Call me tomorrow."

"It'll be too late. Listen to me, man. You know about what went down with your pal Cohen tonight?"

"I heard on the radio there was a shooting at Rondelli's."

"You know who got shot?"

"No. Do you?"

"Yeah. I'm calling from the *Examiner*. They have a scanner in the newsroom. It's all over the cop channels. A big-time bookie named O'Hara, or maybe Whelen, I'm not sure which is his real name—was shot at Cohen's table. Dead. The cops took in everyone for questioning. But right after that, two plain-clothes L.A. cops rousted Jock and me tonight."

Now I was fully awake. "Where?"

"In Toluca Lake. We'd been over there working on Don Johnson's roadster. We were just leaving Les Weingard's when they pulled us over, took us out, shook us down, and tossed my car."

Toluca Lake was a very exclusive gated golf course community adjoining Burbank where Doris Day, Bob Hope, and several of my friends' families lived.

"So, get your registration fixed, pay your tickets. Why're you calling me?"

"Why? You think they were after us? Stevens, come on, get a grip."

"Well, they rousted you, didn't they?"

"I'm a City of L.A. lifeguard. Jock's still in the army, out on furlough. We're so clean we squeak. And they were asking a lot of questions about you. About the whole O'Hara deal. Like we knew shit. They weren't after us, meathead; neither one of us have records. They're trying to find out about you. Thought they'd give us a toss and see if we blabbed."

Suddenly it dawned on me. Lockwood's Ford woody station wagon. It had been parked in front of my old apartment for two nights when he'd had some mechanical trouble. He'd said he'd had to leave it to go back for midterms before he could come back and fix it. *The cops were checking me out.*

"Aw, shit," I groaned. "I'm sor—"

"Save your breath. We have to find out what's going on and how deep they think you're in this. That's why I'm down here at this hour."

"How're you gonna . . ."

"I'll worry about the research; you worry about the retreat."

"Retreat?"

"Time to get strategic, Steve. Everybody you know's talking about this. Dave Carlson called me the other night. Mentioned he'd seen you in Panza's with Cohen. You really want that kind of exposure? Figure out how to get yourself out of this shitstorm before you're a ghost Rider in the sky. Later."

Hanging up, I rolled back over, but sleep didn't come.

Instead, an hour later the phone rang again. I was either going to have to change my number or get new friends. Maybe the second option was best.

"Steve, it's Jock."

Jock Putnam was a close friend from HPS, and Lockwood's former roommate from boarding school. His stepfather was one of Southern California's most distinguished neurosurgeons, and he lived in a virtual castle on a hillside in Beverly Hills. Putnam was just getting out of his U.S. Army reserve service and starting to work in Hollywood as a soundman.

"Yeah, man, what's going on? Can't you guys ever call me at a decent hour?"

"We can't reach you at a decent hour, old boy. You're getting harder and harder to connect with at any hour, decent or indecent. Lockwood tell you what happened to us?"

"Yeah," I groaned wearily.

"Where were you?"

"I was getting laid."

"You know what happened?"

"Not too much. Somebody got shot—I don't know who—and they corralled Uncle Mickey. Say, did I mention I just got another job in a Roger Corman B movie?"

"Oh, shit. There goes your Oscar."

"Dickhead, it's work. I'm leaving town, going to Missouri; can you believe that?"

"Maybe that's a good thing."

"What do you mean?"

"All the guys say you're really getting into this gangster deal."

"Aw, bullshit. Mickey's overrated as a gangster and underrated as a pretty decent guy."

"Steve, c'mon, you think I just fell off the turnip truck? This guy's bad news. You should see what Lockwood dug up on him."

"What're you guys, man? My fuckin' wife? I'm okay, Jock, the world's okay, and you've been worrying for nothing."

"Steve, it's not just me; it's Lockwood, Marc Cavell, Les Weingard, Matteo Muti, Don Duran, Dave Carlson, Larry Beckstead—everybody's really worried. And Big Bertha's Riders, some of the Mouseketeers, like Tommy Cole, buddy, everybody you know."

"Oh, boy, the Riders. Wow. I'm everybody's big deal. Hey, I got news. This isn't HPS, and the Big Bertha's Riders don't mean anything anymore. It was a high-school club. At least these guys are the real deal. Now leave me alone and stop calling when I'm sleeping."

"Listen, Captain Grouch, Dr. Tracy says you should drop by the clinic. He thinks you need some follow-up diagnoses on that head injury."

"Jock, with all due respect, pal, and with all due respect to Dr. Tracy, whom I respect, hang it up and let me get some sleep, huh?"

Jock sucked in his breath. He must've swallowed whatever he was starting to say.

I hung up and turned over to go back to sleep.

But sleep didn't happen. Instead, my mind started churning. If all the people Jock had mentioned were expressing concern, it meant the rumor mill was grinding. Rumors turned into gossip.

And that worried me.

19

HANGOVER

WHEN I FINALLY awakened it was after nine.

My head felt like I'd hired a hamster on a wheel to run my brain. It didn't seem as though I'd had that much to drink. To verify, I checked. The bottle of Bacardi 151 was seriously dented.

Okay, maybe I had. But more likely it was the sure knowledge that last night's close call had been a supreme test of my luck 'n' timing. I'd pushed it—and my stress level—into the red zone on my emotional tachometer. And the Navy doctors in San Diego had warned me about that when I'd been discharged.

I started to light a Parliament but ended up putting the unsmoked cigarette back in the pack. Instead, I pulled on my trunks. Before anything, I needed a quick dip to clear my head. The pool was cool and invigorating, and I toweled off just outside the sliding doors.

On the coffee table was a note from Ashley. *Steve: In Palm Springs for a few days. Make sure you water the plant in the living room. John.*

Housekeeping attended to, I spooned some Folger's into the Sunbeam percolator, pulled on some clothes, and drove down to the big, block-long newsstand on Las Palmas just off Hollywood Boulevard, and gathered up copies of the *Herald Express,* the *Los Angeles Examiner, Daily News, Los Angeles Times,* and the *San Francisco Chronicle*—anything that had a banner line with Mickey Cohen's name in it.

Then I came to my senses and quickly looked around for the *Hollywood Reporter* and *Daily Variety.* I couldn't afford to get that much out of the loop.

Picking up a couple of six-packs at Ralph's—after a subtle request for another autographed Annette photo; the manager never carded me—I drove back to the Lanai and changed back into my damp trunks.

My telephone rang. I ignored it and went out to the pool with my morning coffee, a stack of newspapers, and my neglected Parliament. I needed to figure things out. And a healthy breakfast is important.

I felt apprehensive and wanted to get some perspective on what had happened. Sitting down, I opened the *Examiner,* glanced at the front page and then opened the *Times,* scanned the headlines, and picked up the *Herald Express.*

None of the lead stories agreed with one another. One had a Jack O'Hara, a local bookie, being shot. Another listed the victim as Jack Whelen, a former Air Force officer and military flight instructor; a third called him Jack "the Enforcer" Whelen.

What they all agreed on was that Mickey Cohen was suspected of having some role in the killing of O'Hara/Whelen, and the LAPD was speculating that it had something to do with O'Hara/Whelen's one-man battle against Mickey Cohen; the Sicas; Jack Dragna, a name I'd also heard; and a long list of other suspects and "interested parties" whose names weren't familiar to me.

From overhearing it in several conversations I'd tried not to hear, I recognized O'Hara's name. Joe Sica was the one I'd heard say to Mickey, "It'll be taken care of." Maybe that's what had happened. But why did it happen in a crowded restaurant, with so many witnesses?

A line in one of the articles supplied a clue. Cohen was reputed to be a "silent owner/partner" of Rondelli's.

Whatever it was O'Hara or Whelen had done, it was apparent that during the "taking care of" phase, he'd developed a terminal case of Rondelli's lead poisoning.

Through the open sliding patio door I could hear the phone ring again. Once. Then seconds later, once more. Then seconds later again. The code. I ran in and picked it up.

Lockwood had dug out some more "true gen."

"The victim's real name was Jack Whelen. He was a local. Went to Black Foxx and was a decorated Air Force pilot during the war. Somehow, afterward, he became a successful gentleman's bookie. This pissed one of the syndicate big shots—a guy named Jack Dragna—and Cohen off as he wouldn't tie in with them, and he beat up a couple of Mickey's boys as well as the Sicas when they pushed him."

Black Foxx was an exclusive boys' military academy located in Hollywood, down off Melrose. A couple of years ago, Big Bertha's Riders, after significant fortification with Los Angeles's cheapest local beer, Brew 102, had staged a midnight raid on the school's indoor swimming pool. All of us had gotten caught.

"You heard from Cohen yet? They had to let him go."

"I've been a little hesitant to answer the phone."

"Probably hard to reach from under your bed. Dust bunnies giving you any trouble?"

"Wiseass."

"Be interesting to see what he has to say about all this."

"Yeah, I'll be sure and tell him you asked."

"What you might ask him is how come it took the cops an

hour to get there and why there were no other witnesses in the restaurant."

"I'll pass it on. I'm sure he'll want to know if you're living in the same place."

• • •

My next call was to my father. "Dad, hey, just to let you know that I'm planning to take you guys out for your anniversary day after tomorrow."

"I heard your pal Cohen was involved in some trouble last night. A shooting."

"It's in all the papers."

"But you weren't around, I hope. They hauled them all down for questioning."

"Nope, not me. I had a date."

"We need to talk about that, and your mother."

"Mom? What's the matter?"

"She's—well, her condition's not getting better. I've talked to the doctors. It's going to take some extra attention, and they're going to try some new medication. I don't want her institutionalized."

"I understand. Anything I can do to help? Should we be taking her out?"

"Of course we should; she's your mother, and my wife. The way you help is to be the son you've always been. Love is the best medicine of all. We'll all, you and me, and Reggie—we'll"—he hesitated—"it's going to take a great deal of love and patience. I want to keep her in her normal surroundings, doing normal activities."

"I'll take care of reservations. Okay if I surprise you?"

"I'm sure you'll find a nice place. And Steve, please be careful."

Dad hadn't said it. Not a word. But his concern for me, his pride in what I'd been able to accomplish—on my own in a field he knew from his own hard experience was fraught with disappointment and failure—was in the subtle but cautionary tone of his voice. He loved me, and he would never hold it against me if I weren't a winner. But he didn't want me to make a wrong move and end up a loser.

• • •

The next day, with the newspapers still front-paging the Whelen shooting, I decided to call Mickey's number.

"Yeah, who's this?"

"It's Steve; is that you, Phil?"

"One and only. Where you been, Kid?"

Though there was no edge in Packer's voice, I was still apprehensive—probably oversensitive. I'd been concerned that they might think I'd cut and run, that my occasional casual presence was fair-weather only, and that hearing Mickey'd had trouble had scared me off.

"Hold on, Kid," Phil said. "Mickey wants to talk to you."

I felt my chest tighten.

"Hey, Kid, you okay? 'S'good ya didn't show up the other night, huh? Seems like some guys decided to settle some score right when we were having dinner. The mutherfuckin'cocksuckin'sonofabitch. He deserves dead, whoever the fuck he was."

His ranting was so overboard that I began to suspect it was intended for the ever-present ears of the Los Angeles Police Department's wiretappers.

"W-what happened?" I stammered.

"I never saw a thing. I was in the bathroom, washing my hands. Just as well you and that girl never made it, but where the hell were you?"

I wanted to answer Mickey with phrases that would make me sound as though I were just a casual invite, not one of his retinue. I dropped back to distant-nephew formal.

"Uncle Mickey, thanks so much for the invitation, and I hope you'll understand that I couldn't get near the place. Laurel Canyon was solid traffic both ways; Coldwater was the same. There were police cars everywhere. They had Ventura blocked off going both ways for hours. After being stuck in traffic for two hours, I figured there was no way to get in, and then I heard on the radio there'd been a terrible tragedy. I had to turn down to Moorpark, go all the way down to Sepulveda. Gosh, Uncle Mickey, I'm surely glad you're okay."

I heard his chuckle; he'd gotten my drift. "Sure thing, Kid. Well, feel free to join us over here tomorrow night. You play Hearts?"

"No, sir. It's too hard a game for me, and besides, it's my folks' anniversary. I promised to take them out for dinner."

Suddenly Mickey's voice softened.

"Their anniversary. Yeah? How long?"

"Let's see, twenty years."

"Good, good. What kinda food they like?"

"Dad loves Italian."

"Italian, huh?" He turned away from the phone, and I could hear him speaking to Packer. "Hey, Phil, let's change plans, go to Dino's. It's the Kid's folks' anniversary." Then back to me. "Dino's okay? How's about seven, that early enough for the folks?"

"Perfect, Uncle Mickey," I replied. "My dad's Dean Martin's biggest fan."

"Well, whyn't ya meet us there at seven, and, uh, don't get caught in any traffic."

Was it humor? A slightly sarcastic admonition? I couldn't be sure.

Which, I was beginning to notice, was like a lot of things about my relationship with Mickey Cohen.

20

DINNER AT DINO'S

"**D**AD, LISTEN, I just made reservations for us for tomorrow night at Dino's."

"Dino's? Steve, you shouldn't have."

"Yeah, I should have, Dad. He's your favorite entertainer. I've been subjected to Dean Martin recordings since I can remember. Until I was twelve, I thought he showed up to take showers with you every morning."

"And a good thing, too." Dad chuckled. "Look how well you've turned out."

"So, Dino's at seven. I'll pick you up at six thirty."

In the late 1950s, Dean Martin's well-regarded Sunset Strip restaurant, Dino's, was doubly famous. For all those who lived in Hollywood, it was Mr. Martini's star-studded spot. On any evening, you could find some of entertainment's A-list luminaries there, as well as members of Frank Sinatra's famous clan, the so-called Rat Pack, including Sammy Davis Jr., Peter Lawford, Joey Bishop, and Shirley MacLaine.

But to the rest of America, Dino's shared a driveway with *77*

MEL, SALLY, AND STEVE STEVENS.

Sunset Strip, a hugely popular quasi-suave detective TV series starring Efrem Zimbalist Jr. and Roger Smith, as well as occasional guest spots by Connie Stevens, another schoolmate from Hollywood Professional School who was already a singing star in her own right, with a chart-topping R&R record, "Sixteen Reasons," and the big hit novelty song "Kookie, Kookie, Lend Me Your Comb," as well as a starring role as "Cricket" in the other big TV detective show, *Hawaiian Eye.*

About the only thing missing as we pulled up to Dino's was the "Kookie" car-parking character who was played on the show by Edd Byrnes. As a consolation prize, however, all the red-jackets sported near-identical Edd Byrnes–style haircuts.

"Steve," said my dad with his wry sense of humor and ever-observant eye, "do you think these guys all have the same barber?"

Dad was obviously delighted being here, and his enthusiasm was infectious. We both took Mom's arms, and dad winked at me as we matched steps and entered through the two big doors.

"Nice footwork, son. That's the best high-roller entrance I've made all day."

"Not bad," I said, "and speaking of high rollers, while we're here, there's someone I'd like you to meet."

Dad's eyebrows rose as he looked at me, but by this time we were standing in front of Mickey, Joe Sica, and an elegant-looking, matronly woman whom I'd never seen. Mickey and Fred stood. The older woman, it turned out, was Joe's wife.

Mickey took center stage, gestured for everyone to sit, and motioned the waiter to pour wine. Mickey lifted his glass. "So, a toast to Mr. and Mrs. Stevens on this special occasion. We won't need menus tonight. Mr. Stevens, when your son told me you were having your anniversary and you was a big fan of Dino, I called and asked the chef to make his specialty for you."

And as if on cue, Dean Martin appeared at the side of the table. "Mickey, Mickey. How's it hangin', baby?"

"Hanging? Dino, what's new in this town? As usual, they're trying to hang something on me I never done."

Martin shook his head and smiled. "Sounds like you were in the wrong Italian restaurant at the wrong time. You better start coming here more often. But Mickey, you know my maître d's gonna make you check all the hardware at the door."

Mickey loved it. Even Joe laughed. Mrs. Sica made eye contact with Mom, and they both shook their heads in a boys-will-be-boys gesture.

Dad's expressions ranged from puzzlement to delight with this exchange. And he gave me a little punch on my shoulder.

Mickey, our evening's impresario, said grandly, "Now, Dino, the real reason we are all here tonight is this lovely couple, Mel and Sally, the parents of this young actor, here. It's their twentieth anniversary."

Dean Martin leaned over, shook Dad's and my hands, and kissed Mom on the cheek. "Mr. Martin," I said, "Dad's such a fan of your singing that I grew up thinking our alarm clock was synced to 'About a Quarter to Nine.'"

"His memory's slipping," Dad retorted. "It's either 'Carolina in the Morning,' 'I Got the Sun in the Morning,' or 'Good Morning, Life.' Then I have the nighttime songs."

Martin pointed to my dad. "For fans like this, Mickey, dinner's on the house."

My father stood up to thank him, and Dean extended both hands to him. Cohen may have bought the dinner, but there was no money on heaven or earth that could have bought Martin's spontaneous and genuine outpouring of warmth and charm.

Sitting down, my mother, lucid and every bit the vivacious Judy Holliday pixie we all had been missing, patted my dad's arm. "Mel and I have known a few people the government tried to hang things on."

Dad caught my quick glance. Uh-oh.

Cohen's ears perked up. "The government—ha—it oughtta be illegal."

"That's just what Mr. Capone used to say." My mother

dropped this bomb as she demurely dabbed the corner of her mouth with her napkin.

"No. No kiddin'? You knew Big Al?"

"Why, Mr. Cohen, did I know Mr. Alphonse Capone? I was in the first speakeasy I'd ever been in—that was back in Chicago, of course—when it was raided. Everybody was panicking and then I felt a tap on my shoulder, and next to me was Mr. Capone. I had no idea who he was; he just looked like a very-well-dressed gentleman. He handed me a great big pistol and said, 'The cops will search me for certain, but they'll just chase you out the door because you're so young. Can you hide this under your dress for me?'

"Well, I still had no idea who he was, but I said I would, and just as he'd predicted, the police made all the women leave, and searched the men."

Mickey was leaning forward, mouth slightly open, listening intently.

"I was standing outside," Mom continued, "not knowing what on earth to do with this huge gun, when he finally came out and started to get into this enormous black Lincoln. I called out: 'Mister! Over here!' And he looked around and spotted me. I walked right up to that big car and handed him the pistol wrapped up in my silk scarf. He was so surprised he leaned inside, and the men up front rolled down the windows to look.

"'You're a sweet kid, and here's a hundred dollars,' he said, and he pinched my cheek. So I told him I didn't mind him asking me for a favor, and I didn't need the money—even though I really did—but that I just wanted him to promise me he wouldn't shoot anyone with it.

"And he looked right at me, put his hand on his heart, and said, 'Little missy, I promise you, I'll never shoot anybody who doesn't need shooting.'"

Mickey roared. "That's terrific. That's just like Big Al. Did you ever see him again?"

"Mickey," Mom regaled him, "he was living in the Hotel Metropole in Chicago. He had several floors, and as luck would have it, I ended up, a few weeks after applying for and getting a job in the florist's shop, down in the lobby. He came in one morning, spotted me, and called me over.

"'Little missy, I remember you,'" Mom quoted, into the Chicago accent. "'You brung me luck once, and you'll do it again.' After that he wouldn't let any of the other girls make up his white carnation boutonnieres."

"He was a very swanky dresser, wasn't he?" Mickey was enthralled.

"Say what you want about Mr. Capone, but he was always polite, well-tailored, and I never saw him without his hat and cane."

"You know," Mickey waxed nostalgic, "they got us both for income-tax evasion? Mickey and Big Al."

"Oh, I actually saw those federal agents come into the hotel and . . ."

I felt Dad's toe tap my ankle under the table. I was pretty sure my mother had never met Al Capone, but her descriptions and details were so real and her stories so vivid that I started to wonder if maybe she was telling the truth.

When the dessert cart came Mrs. Sica turned to me. "Joe and Fred have both told me about your acting career, and that you have worked with Annette on a number of occasions."

"You couldn't ask for a better person to work with," I assured her.

"That's *so* wonderful to hear nice things about such a beautiful Italian girl. Does she break all the boys' hearts?"

"We all love her, Mrs. Sica. She's such a doll. We think of her as our sister."

"I have a niece named Annette. Do you think it would be possible to get an autographed picture for her?"

"Of course. I'll give it to Joe the next time I see him."

Mickey reached over and wagged his finger. "We'll be at the Brown Derby on Vine, tomorrow about one. C'mon by."

"You got it, Uncle Mickey," I acknowledged.

• • •

Life strikes some funny poses. Driving my parents home, I stole a glance at my straight-arrow dad, his arm around my mother, leaning against the Pontiac's passenger door and looking as contented as I'd seen him in many years—an honest guy who crossed all his legal *t*'s and dotted all his legal *i*'s—who'd just spent a delightful evening in the company of a known gangland figure, an ex-con, and, if the newspapers were right, a cold-blooded killer.

He noticed my glance as we stopped at the light on Highland.

"Makes you wonder, doesn't it, Steve, if a guy like Dean Martin befriends a man like Mickey, can he be all bad?"

At nineteen, I still hadn't learned what success, however it's measured by men as dissimilar as Dean Martin and Mickey Cohen, teaches early—that nobody's all bad or all good, and one can use the other when the need arises.

21

BROWN DERBY DILEMMA

IN HOLLYWOOD IN those days, there were places—and there were "places."

The Brown Derby was a "place." Located just below Hollywood Boulevard on the east side of Vine Street and just down from the stately brown-brick Taft Building, it had a vaguely Moroccan facade reminiscent of Rick's Café Americain in the film *Casablanca*.

Pulling into the 25¢ Auto Park lot across the street, I waited for a break in traffic on Vine Street and sprinted across.

Walking into the Brown Derby, I stopped while the hostess seated a couple in front of me. I had an odd kind of reverse déjà vu. For more than a year I'd stood on the other side of the white plaster walls, looking in through the curtained windows. But I'd never been inside. My parents had never taken me, nor, as I was then, would I have been allowed in the door.

Founded by silent-film star Gloria Swanson's husband, it was—like the Musso & Frank Grill—a very "Hollywood" part of Hollywood, and unlike today's Hollywood, no one with a modicum of self-respect would have even thought of entering wearing "urban" styles and sporting facial stubble. And this applied to studio executives and gangsters alike.

Mickey, Joe, Fred, Phil, and Joey D. may have been classic gangsters, but they were suit-and-tie gangsters. Hair neatly trimmed, shoes always shined, and looking generally well put together—if not to the prevailing Ivy League standards of the day—they tended to favor somewhat more flamboyant, custom-tailored garments from such star-grade tailors as Sy Devore and Mel Wise.

Today, the use of *gangster* as a descriptive noun has gone out of fashion. Today we hear only the collective "Ebonic" noun *gangstas,* and it denotes the worst kind of detritus—social disposables who seem willing to sink to new lows given the least encouragement or occasion. Sure, we still have the Mafia, but by comparison they're GQ fashion plates.

THE BROWN DERBY ON HOLLYWOOD AND VINE.

For young men of my age, the preppy/Ivy League look was both fashionable and stylish. Button-down blue, pink, and white oxford-cloth shirts from Brooks Brothers; narrow rep, regimental, or knit ties. I'd recently purchased a pair of slim-fitting Cambridge gray flannels; a narrow-lapelled, three-button Harris Tweed sport jacket without shoulder pads; and cordovan Bass Weejuns penny loafers with Argyle socks from Zeidler & Zeidler, a trendy traditional-style men's shop next to Schwab's Drugstore on Sunset and Crescent Heights.

And that's how I looked when the hostess led me back to find Mickey, passing George Burns and Gracie Allen in one booth and Burt Lancaster and a party of studio types in another. Mickey and Joe were sitting in a large and very private back booth. As they moved over for me, I could see people leaning out of their booths, hoping to catch a glimpse of Mickey. His love of notoriety and publicity had obviously been given a boost since the Whelen murder.

Mickey, however, was appraising me.

"Nice threads, Kid. That's a very good look on you; very sharp."

"Uncle Mickey, I used to stand on the corner right outside," I said, pointing, "selling newspapers and watching nicely dressed people coming in here and wondering what it was like."

"You? You sold papers?" Mickey seemed incredulous. He looked at Joe as if to confirm the ridiculousness of such a claim. "When? When'd you sell papers?"

"When I was thirteen. And I had a tough fight getting and keeping the corner."

Sica looked even more doubtful.

"Jesus, Kid, you were a newsboy. No wonder I liked you right away. We got a lot in common. I sold papers downtown, right here. I learned how to hustle doing that. Guys'd leave little 'packages' for other guys, y'know, Pro'bishun 'n' all that. I'd get a whole quarter tip. Sometimes, when I got a kinda dumb guy I knew was coming to pick up, I'd hide it around the corner. He'd come up and ask, and I'd tell him some other guy got it but I knew where another bootlegger was, and I'd get him another bottle. Then I'd go get his, and he'd pay me for it and give me a tip."

"Well, Uncle Mickey, I remember yelling, 'EXTRA, EXTRA, READ ALL ABOUT IT! MICKEY COHEN ACQUITTED OF ASSAULT CHARGES!'" I laughed. It was a lie.

"Yeah, well, did you ever pull the old trick—"

I interrupted. "You mean, yelling, 'EXTRA, EXTRA!' when there was no extra edition out and nothing to read at all? You bet."

Mickey laughed and slapped me on the back. "Kid, that brings back great memories."

Mickey's burst of nostalgia must have prompted some hidden palm dirt, and he got up to go wash his hands. Joe watched him for a few moments and then turned to me with great concern in his eyes.

"The Missus, she's a little concerned about something."

"Oh, about the photo of Annette for your niece? I have to go over to the studio and pick it up when she's there to autograph it." It seemed like a reasonable explanation, but it was soon obvious that it was anything but.

"Well, Kid, look, da' udda night we was kiddin' ya about Annette, askin' if you was bangin' her. We all talked it over. And, honestly, Kid, we was way off base wit' dat. You made it clear—she's a nice Italian girl, a Catholic girl, a virgin as she should be till marriage. What I din't at this time know was how much the Italian community has great reference an' respect for this young girl. I was kiddin' wit' my niece, an' she was very offended, as she tinks da worlt of Annette. And it was right you standin' up fa' her honor like that."

"I, uh . . . ," I began, but before I could voice my thought, Joe was drowning me in contrition.

"You don' haveta make no excuses. Sayin' that you respected her, not even admittin' you was seein' her, but that you was jus' perfessional. That tolt us all somethin' about youse we din't know. You got good morals, an' we all respect that, what ya done. Good morals is important in this game. Unnerstand?"

I had to yank my jawbone out of my lap. Joe had never spoken a sentence longer than a few words to me. Now I was receiving confession.

"Joe, honestly, Annette's just a good friend, and I work on her series professionally."

Steve Stevens is often seen with Annette when Paul is away but she doesn't limit her dates to him nor anyone else exclusively. Who will win the battle for Annette's heart? At the moment it is anyone's guess.

THE word is out: Paul Anka is real bugged with Annette Funicello.

"I leave town, and a new guy moves in. I don't get it," Paul said to a pal. Well, Paul, you being a headstrong kind of a guy wouldn't realize that Annette is young, and that she's testing her love for you.

"I like Paul a lot," Annette said, "but I like other fellows, too." Other fellows can be narrowed down to one guy in particular. His name is Steve Stevens.

"I dig Annette," Steve says, "and I'll see her whenever she says yes to my asking her out."

Paul figured he was top dog with Annette when he went out on a personal appearance tour of various Eastern cities. Then, he comes back to Hollywood, and a buddy tells him Annette's been seeing a lot of Steve Stevens.

Paul was ready to start swinging, but cooler heads prevailed. They reminded him that he'd cut Fabian out as head man with Annette, and that Steve was only pushing his luck with Annette.

"Annette's a funny girl," one of her girl friends said, "she wants to be so sure of the fellow she marries that she'll get him a little sore (continued on page 74)

TV & SCREEN LIFE

19

"Ex'atly. Just what I was sayin'. I unnerstan'. An' I respect you for this, but see, the missus was to the dentis' this morning, an' she was reading in one of them Hollywood magazines, *TV and Screen Life,* and now there's some concern that this Greek fuck is tryin' ta steal Annette from you."

"Greek fuck? Which Greek fuck?"

"Anka. That greasy Greek fuck, Paul Anka. I don' even like the way he sings. So, you want we should take care of this, we'll do him."

"Joe, whoa, that's so—" I had to stop to find the right word. This was suddenly a major vocabulary challenge.

How could I politely refuse this generous and very concerned offer to bump off a major young entertainment talent in order to defend a nonexistent love relationship with a colleague—a relationship that had been fabricated by a movie-mag flack—and not hurt Joe's feelings or imply that I was disputing Mrs. Sica's motivation to provide Italian-American youth with a virtuous female role model?

"Joe—that's so *considerate* of you. I really appreciate it. And if Annette's friendship with me goes any farther, and someone gets in the way, I'll take you up on it. But honestly, that's just Hollywood PR bullshit. Guys sit in offices in New York, in front of typewriters with cups of coffee and pastrami sandwiches, making this shit up. They never actually meet us. It's all just make-believe. I met Anka a few times, and he seems to be a straight-up guy."

"But what do I tell the missus? She's bought a loada shit in that magazine?"

Oops, cognitive dissonance. Contradicting the supposed authority of the printed word, especially in gossip magazines that most of the United States took as gospel, required some deft verbal footwork.

"Just tell her they don't know what they're talking about and not to worry."

Mickey returned, waving and greeting people as he passed through the room. "Okay, Kid," he said, sliding into the booth. "I need you to do me a favor. You got time tonight?"

"Sure, Uncle Mickey. What is it?" *Please don't make me pick up that sick pervert again,* I prayed.

"Here," he said, handing me a piece of paper wrapped in two one-hundred-dollar bills. "I need you to pick up a package and take it to a friend of mine. Okay? The dough's gas money. We can always trust a newsboy, right, Joe?"

Joe nodded. "Maybe we drop 'Kid,' start callin' him 'the Newsboy'?"

Great, I thought to myself . . .

EXTRA, EXTRA!
ACTOR STEVE "THE NEWSBOY" STEVENS
BUSTED IN GANGLAND SCHEME!

22

WESTLAKE WALTZ

MOONLIGHT, THE KIND Southern California locals call "Hollywood Moonlight," was splattering lunar silver on the street when I pulled out of the Fountain Lanai's garage and headed down Highland Avenue.

My first destination—on Pico, south of MacArthur Park—wasn't an area I knew well. Jock Putnam and I had visited a strip club on Pico near Normandie. But that was about it. And the only reason we'd even thought about going was that Lockwood—the perennial "I'll take any work anywhere, anytime" college student—had played a gig there once and put out the word that the place would serve anyone over twelve.

It was definitely a factor that compensated for the seediness of the surroundings, and the stretch marks on the aging strippers. That was good enough for Jock, who, in his inimitable fashion, soon made friends with the bouncer.

I stayed on Highland, driving south past Santa Monica, Melrose, and Beverly Boulevards to Wilshire Boulevard, turned left and then headed east, past Western and Vermont Avenues. At

Hoover Avenue, Wilshire jogs right and becomes a wide, palm-studded overpass that bisects the lake.

Designed in the 1880s, Westlake Park had been rechristened MacArthur Park in 1946. But Hollywood old-timers always called the still-beautiful lake "Westlake," the name it was known by when Westlake Village—just west of today's downtown Los Angeles—was an elegant meeting place. The shallow lake was bordered with stately one-hundred-foot-high Washingtonian and the Hollywood-trademark Canary Islands palms, and a variety of shade trees that canopied the park's serpentine pathways.

Attractive as it looked in daylight, at night it had recently started slipping. Now its main nocturnal attraction was attracting the unattractive.

Passing through the park, I turned right on Alvarado and headed south to where it joined Hoover. Hoover crossed Pico, and I made a left turn. The address was a small storefront dry cleaner in a row of shops that dated from the 1920s.

Getting out, I locked the convertible. Not that it would stop a fast hand with a sharp knife. This neighborhood was in transition—the kind of transition that has the adjective "urban" prefixed to it but is not suffixed by "renewal." That "urban" meant bad things for real-estate values and an upsurge in spray-paint sales.

Two doors down I spotted the address. A sign announced that Champion Cleaners was closed—maybe since 1941, from the way it looked. After my third three-beat knock on the dirty glass door, a light appeared through a door behind the counter. A thickset figure appeared—backlit—and then the door closed. Now I was backlit by the moonlight and the streetlight a few yards away. I could tell I was being once-overed.

A dead bolt snapped back, and the door opened the whole three inches its security chain allowed. Towering over me was a man with a severely pockmarked face, and an ear that could have sold as yesterday's cauliflower at the Hollywood Ranch Market. He didn't have "washed-up heavyweight" stenciled on his dirty T-shirt, but it was probably only a wardrobe oversight.

"Yeah? Whatcha want? We're closed." The warmth of his greeting was diminished only by the threatening thrust of his lower lip.

My inner-wiseass couldn't resist.

"*Ring Magazine* sent me to do a 'Where Is He Now?' profile."

"Huh?" I could hear the security chain strain against the doorjamb. "Whatcha say?"

"Our mutual friend sent me to pick up a package." Mentioning Mickey's name didn't seem necessary. I had the impression that the Champ had been waiting patiently since Mickey's last threatening phone call. Probably forgot to go down within ten seconds after the ref told him to shake hands and come out fighting.

"Oh, yeah," he grunted. "Okay. Hang on."

I turned my back to the door, hung on, and studied the street. It was just after nine, and traffic was thin. I was beginning to realize that being a tuff guy was harder at night on a street like this than it was on Sunset Boulevard.

The only car in fifty yards was parked across Pico—a ratty-looking 1949 Hudson convertible, top up, with a dented left-front fender and its hood tied down with a wire coat hanger. This wasn't the worst neighborhood in L.A., but it wasn't Franklin and Gower, either, and—given the car I was driving and the way I was dressed—I was definitely from somewhere west of Western Avenue. Still, so far, so good. My life of crime might be relegated to being a well-dressed delivery boy, but what the hell. I was meeting interesting people.

From inside the store I could hear a phone ring once. Minutes passed, then Punchy reappeared, cracked the door, and handed me a leather satchel slightly larger than a woman's large handbag.

"Thanks," I said. "See you at the Olympic, you can autograph my fight card." And walked the thirty feet to my car.

Cocky, huh?

Getting in, I happened to glance across the street. There were two black shapes inside the Hudson. I hadn't noticed them before, and suddenly something didn't feel right. I felt a moment's panic, and waited for it to subside. It didn't.

At HPS, Major Goddard, the drama teacher, stressed riding the prevailing emotional reaction to a line or another actor's action to drive your part in the scene. Just recalling that gave me a tiny moment of clarity.

I started up, but before turning on my lights, I cranked the wheel all the way left with my left foot hard on the brake and my right halfway down on the accelerator, and the Pontiac's tach reading 3,500. Catching a break in traffic, I flicked on the headlights, goosed it, and spun a fishtailing U-turn.

I had the green-turning-yellow on Pico, and it was only a few hundred feet to the Hoover intersection, but as I straightened out I saw lights come on behind me. One was pointing high, as if from a damaged left-front fender. Then I heard a screech of tires. That Hudson ran the red light.

Aw, shit. It was the oldest B-movie setup in the world.

Crook A—sent by the Big Boss—arrives for the pickup.

Crook B hands over the ill-gotten gains.

Crook A takes off. Only to be followed and waylaid by Crooks C and D, who relieve Crook A of the ill-gotten gains, and in the process perhaps inflict upon him bodily harm, or worse, and disappear into the night.

Crook A then drags his sorry Crook A ass back to the Big Boss with his story.

Big Boss calls Crook B, who tells him, "Don't blame me. Ask your boy. I handed off as expected."

Big Boss now has the option of believing Crook A, or not. And since Big Boss is Big Boss, a position he arrived at in the Criminal World by being skeptical of stories of missing dough, will surely inflict upon Crook A the requisite bodily harm.

But I was an actor, and my car wasn't a tractor. I could drive pretty well, and I'd seen enough Robert Mitchum/Raymond Chandler movies to know that if you make four right turns in a row and the suspect crook-car is still behind you, ergo, you are being followed.

All of which I did dutifully, and ascertained with proficiency—when I turned back onto Pico heading west—that the crook-car was hot on my tail.

Again, *Aw, shit!*

This wasn't in the script. I started doing quick calculations: $200 for pickup and delivery. Scale plus $75. Combat pay? Well, if there was more to come, it wouldn't come unless I delivered.

While my car was certainly faster and I could easily outrun them, I was operating under rules-of-engagement. I had a bag, probably containing many thousands of dollars or something worth many thousands, to deliver.

If the cops stopped me, they'd search. They'd get the dollars, I'd get a trip downtown, a good Jack Webb–ing, and at the very least a night in jail. Unless the satchel contained something worth not only many thousands of dollars, but many nights in jail as well.

I'd miss my goddamn flight to Kansas City, and my chance to play a dork in *High School Caesar.* A role I was wondering now if I wasn't more than adequately cut out for.

After that?

Well, I was getting the distinct impression that fucking up Uncle Mickey's deals by bringing the heat down on my head, and by association on his head, at a time when there was already plenty of dead-bookie heat on the Cohen coterie's collective heads, might spoil my chance to die in bed, a rich and successful actor with a long line of credits and Oscars, at ninety.

Aw, shit. They were closing in on me.

Discretion favored the bed-at-ninety option. That meant playing it cool, smart, practical, and tactical—losing these bastards without screwing up. I made a legal right with the greenie on Vermont Avenue. It was about twenty blocks to the Hollywood Freeway where I could use car-power to elude pursuit.

But now they were less than a block behind me, and I'd just made the light at Melrose. Traffic was light enough to weave in and out but avoid using my turn-signals. On my left I could see the campus and buildings of Los Angeles City College, and just ahead of me a bus was pulling out from the curb.

Scooting in front of the bus masked my next move—I hung a tight right. Glancing up, I noticed the street sign—Lockwood Avenue. *Luck 'n' timing.* It had to be a good omen—friends were looking out for me—psychic remote control.

Coincidences were nice, but concealment was better. And that's what I needed now.

Going a block farther I saw several large buildings, killed my headlights, and pulled into Lockwood Elementary School's service parking area behind an L.A. City Board of Education truck that was unloading what appeared to be furniture.

Waiting for a few minutes—watching to see if by any chance they'd followed me—proved a relief. Nothing. Breathing easier, I pulled onto North Virgil, headed toward Santa Monica Boulevard, got back on Vermont and then onto the Hollywood Freeway.

Whew. I fished a Parliament out of my now-soaking-wet shirt pocket and pushed in the cigarette lighter. My drop-off address was fairly near, on Sunset, just a matter of eight or ten blocks away. Right-O. Clever chap. Practically home-free.

But no sooner had I taken my first deep drag than I spotted what looked like that cockeyed headlight in my rearview mirror.

Aw, shit!

Goosing it again, my faithful big-cube, four-barrel, OHV leaped ahead, and they were left behind.

Until I hit Highland Avenue

Where a bus blocked the right turn lane.

And a solid line of cars blocked my attempt to thread the needle and make a left when the light finally changed.

With the Hudson directly behind me now, I could see that there were more than just two heads. *Aw, shit, squared.*

Bravado, where are you now that I need you? Bravado was off in the wings somewhere, so I settled for terror, spiced with a healthy dose of panic and topped with gut-wrenching fear. Mickey? I'd deal with him later; now it was these guys, whoever they were. And my face being my fortune—or so since my recent twentieth birthday, I believed—I didn't figure having it prematurely bear the marks of experience—bad experience.

I jammed into the first alley I could find south of Sunset, roared through a few more, headed down Santa Monica, jumped a curb into the Farmer's Market parking lot, roared out on Fairfax, headed north to Sunset again, and came to ground in the parking lot of Ben Frank's Restaurant, a landmark drive-in coffee shop that never closed.

My heart was beating so hard that it gave a whole new physiological dimension to tachycardia.

Grabbing the satchel, I double-timed it inside, elbowed my way through the dense pack of waiting patrons, and found the phone bank.

Dialing Mickey's number proved to be a digital disaster. I couldn't get the numbers in the correct sequence. On the third try I got it right, and hearing Phil Packer brought my heart rate down to a diastolic drumroll.

"Kid, you sound funny. You okay?"

"I—I—got Mickey's package, Phil. But I got set up and tailed. I thought I lost 'em, but they found me again. And then—"

"Yeah, yeah, but where're you now?"

"Ben Frank's, on the Strip. Eighty-five-hundred block. I—"

"Good. You stay put. Don't do nothin'. Don't go out until we come to get you. Hear?"

"Yeah, this place is crowded. Do you think—"

"Nah. Sit right at the counter. Get a coffee. Somebody'll be right over."

I found a seat at the counter that gave me a good view of the entrance. Everyone entering looked suspicious—and then an unkempt, sleazy-looking guy in dirty clothes wormed his way in past the hostess and headed straight toward me. Clutching the satchel in a death grip, I tightened my hand around the solid bulk of the coffee mug, prepared to use it the way Mickey had used that champagne bottle.

If he was looking for me, Dirtbag's straining bladder must have been his highest priority. He never saw me—just headed past, beelining it for the restrooms. And right behind him, like John Wayne and the Cavalry, were Itchy and Fred. I tossed a buck on the counter and joined them.

Outside, they walked me toward my car, and, spotting the Hudson ragtop, I pointed. Inside were two men, smoking. Neither had noticed me.

Fred held his index finger to his lips. "Don't say nuthin', and don't worry about them. You go on. We'll take care a' it."

Still shaking from adrenaline saturation, I climbed back into my car and started the engine. As I pulled out I could see Fred, trying to pound some sense into the miscreants' heads.

From the looks of the clumps of hair and smears of blood on the old Hudson's dented door and rear quarter panel, he was having some success.

He was no doubt instructing them to avoid interfering with Uncle Mickey's newsboy.

23

BIRDS OF A FEATHER

Rolling out of bed early the next morning, I realized that time was getting short, Christmas was approaching, and I'd be going on location for a month soon after that.

On one hand, that sounded great. I'd be visiting a part of the country I'd never seen, working on a picture with several old pals, and making new contacts. But there was another factor, a cluster of mixed emotions I hadn't quite been able to put words around.

Hanging out with Uncle Mickey was kind of neat. That macho part of me loved the power Mickey and his boys radiated. It was the same feeling I'd had in the Marine Corps. I was part of something bigger, tougher, more powerful than I. An entity that accepted me, gave me membership, provided for me, and with whom I broke my bread.

Well, Villa Capri wasn't exactly a mess hall. And anybody who's ever ridden forty miles on a Camp Pendleton exercise on the wooden slat seats of a duce-and-a-half wearing a full compliment of field-gear would no doubt settle for a Caddy Brougham, but the psychological similarities were there.

And even I was beginning to see them.

While my acting career was progressing, I wasn't under contract to a studio. I was depending on an agent who had another twenty actors in my age range. I had to audition; contract actors had screen tests. I paid my own bills; they had business managers.

And there were times when—while I wasn't broke—I was having to either dip into my meager reserves or go on unemployment to pay those bills.

Self-indulgence was part of the equation. Because of the money I earned as a young actor, I'd been able to attend a Hollywood private school. I had friends whose parents lived on estates in Beverly Hills. I'd had plenty of opportunity as a kid to see the differences between what my parents' adequate but limited middle-class income provided and what real money could provide. And a part of me—the part that housed my talent, my ego, my drive to succeed—felt I was entitled to some of that.

And while I hadn't fully identified the importance of this half-realized insight and dealt with it, I knew subconsciously that this was the part that liked being around Mickey. He was who he was, did what he did, and took no shit from anybody. Sure, he'd done time, but he never complained. I'd heard him say it: "You fuck up, you pay." You couldn't put it more concisely than that.

In this real-life movie, Mickey Cohen was both producer and director. He'd auditioned me, and now he was invested in my playing the part he'd assigned. The trouble was, I wasn't quite sure what the role he'd selected really required. I was working scene-by-scene, off pages of a script I'd never fully read.

Just then the phone rang. My agent, more talkative than usual, a phenomenon I'd noticed when there was a part in the offing. Why not? I got a part—he got a cut.

"The show's called *The Target: Corruptors,* and it looks like a good part. They'll call back to confirm."

I still had the two hundred dollars Mickey had given me—

equal to roughly a thousand dollars today. But I also still had to let Mickey know what had happened last night, and see if I'd handled the situation correctly.

With money to spare this week, I stopped at Tiny Naylor's Drive-In on Sunset for breakfast. With the convertible's top down, a beautiful, warm Southern California day unfolding, and four cups of coffee motivating me to take care of business, I headed west to Brentwood, and Mickey's.

Itchy answered the door, and when I walked in I saw the fat guy I'd met some weeks before.

"C'mon in, Kid. Mickey's on a run; he'll be back in a couple of hours. You can hang around if you feel like it."

"Long enough to thank you for pulling my ass outta that jam last night?"

"Hey, you did good. We told Mickey, and he's proud the way you handled it. You were smart to get close by and go to that restaurant. If you'd gone to the drop-off, they could have taken you and the other party, too. That would have been bad for business. But we sent you out without backup, and you proved you could handle it. Frankly, Kid, you should have had some heat. For this, I blame myself."

"Thanks, Itchy, but you shouldn't. I wanted to square that away with Mickey, and let him know that I got what looks like a great part."

"That's terrific Kid. You give him a call. He loves to hear stuff about your career."

"Career"? From Itchy?

As I started for the door he put his hand on my shoulder. The way he was standing blocked the Fat Man's view of me. In his right hand was a little five-shot, snub-nosed .32 Smith & Wesson revolver.

"You need to carry this when you make a run. It's just a little insurance, so if what happened last night happens again—well, you have a little protection."

Placing it in my hand, he smiled as if he'd just handed me a Little League trophy. *Best First Game Rookie.* I hefted it. It was actually a little heavier than it looked, but it was no Colt .38 Super 1911 A-1 automatic, like the two Itchy carried in right-and-left shoulder holsters, not to mention the .38 Colt Chief's Special he carried in an ankle holster.

I found myself unable to adequately respond. I'd just been given an award. It wasn't an Oscar, but it might be an Emmy. Or a merit badge.

A .32 was a ladies' purse gun. A little more power than a .22 or a .25. Itchy didn't know I'd been a Marine, that I knew what serious man-stopping weaponry was like. But he hadn't insulted me, either; .32 belly guns like this had claimed plenty of cheating husbands' lives.

"Thanks, Itchy," I said, unable to think of anything better. I didn't want to offend him. It was obviously Itchy's way of telling me he cared. But tender sentiment aside, I didn't even know if I wanted to carry a gun.

"I appreciate it, Itchy," I said. "Sure wish I'd had this last night. Would have saved me a phone call." And shook his hand.

Dropping the gun into my jacket pocket, I left.

24

CHALK TALK

"**S**TEVE, HEY. YOU'RE home." JOHN Ashley kneed open the front door and piled a load of shopping bags on the bar. He seemed genuinely delighted to encounter another living being in this two-bedroom fifteen-hundred-square-foot apartment.

"No shit, Sherlock," I said, looking up from the well-thumbed and marked-up *High School Caesar* script I'd been studying. "I haven't seen you since I moved in. My rent check for the last month is still in your stack of unopened mail."

"Tonight's your night. I'm balled-out."

"Been on a one-man perpetual pussy patrol?"

Ashley rolled his eyes. "I'm a man whose sexual appetites are assuaged, whose carnal knowledge is verging on encyclopedic, who's managed to short-circuit his compelling male sexo-electromagnetism—whose dick is plumb wore out, hoss. I need nourishment. And here it is! I brung home the bacon, the beans, and"—he lifted one brown paper bag and a six-pack of Coors poked through the damp corner—"the booze."

"And the cook, Shakespeare?"

"You?"

"Negative. Stevens smokes, Stevens drinks, Stevens parties, Stevens is neat and tidy. But Stevens don't cook."

"Well, that settles that. We'll get some takeout. Barbecue okay?" he asked, dialing Barney's Beanery, the popular Santa Monica Boulevard actors' hangout. "Want a suds?"

I settled for my favorite, rum and Coke, glad for the chance to talk to Ashley about the film and my part—which I thought might be the role that could turn my career around.

Ashley popped the cap on a Coors and listened to my questions. When the deliveryman from Barney's arrived, we knocked off to fall on the mesquite-smoked baby back ribs like a couple of herd-driving cowhands from *Gunsmoke*.

Popping another Coors, Ashley confided his estimate of the film's chances. "Here's the way I look at it. The script's so-so. But we've got the chance as actors to really make it stretch. The lead character I'm playing, Matt Stevens, is a dyed-in-the wool sociopath."

"What's that mean?" I asked. It wasn't a term I was familiar with. Ashley was older, and he had been to college and studied other subjects besides acting.

"He's a guy without a shred of conscience. He's a user. He mistreats those who are close to him. He'll screw anybody, and yet while all his buddies know it, they still remain loyal to him, even as he gets them in deeper and deeper. The other kids in the high school fear him; he's rich, without any restrictions, and he's a powerful personality."

John took the script and thumbed through it.

"Here, this is about fifteen minutes into it. I've just rigged getting elected to student body president and we're in the local teen-hangout burger joint. I've just told everybody I'm going to continue holding the Friday night dances, but it's going to cost two bits to get in. I've got all these little rackets going. Nobody likes the idea of paying, but I tell them, 'Look, it's going to go for buying a mascot. Since we're the Wilson High Bulldogs, it's going to be a little bulldog puppy.'"

I took the script back. "Yeah, right here. The 'Steve' character says: 'You can bet there's some catch if he has anything to do with it.'"

"Right. They've got his number, but he's got theirs as well."

"What about my character? How do you see him?"

"Cricket's a tagalong. He's not so much a dork as he is a basically nice little dumbass guy who's trying to be cool. But he doesn't really know how, and he looks up to my character, who sees him as just another pawn."

"Sorta the classic tragic character?"

"All the other guys in my character Matt's gang have leather jackets. You don't. They're all bigger guys; you're small. They don't smile, they sneer; you—" John thought for a moment. "How do you see yourself playing this?"

"Kinda Jerry Lewis. Geeky. I never have good clothes. I do jerky little moves and gestures, clown but don't get seen as very funny. Something like that."

"Good. I was afraid you were going to go for Sal Mineo in *Rebel*. Believe me, Caesar may be without a cause, but it's no Rebel, and I'm no James Dean."

"How does Cricket relate to Matt?"

"Well, you want to be like Matt, but you can't quite figure out what it takes. So you always let down. Then you bounce back, like a cute little puppy, but that makes you look weak, and you resent it."

"Yeah. I hadn't quite figured out his motivation, but okay. That's good."

We continued on for another few minutes, and I could sense that Ashley was getting restless.

"Listen, it's a neat night," he finally said. "Why don't we take your car, put down the top, cruise the Boulevard, and see if it looks like there's any action at the Red Velvet." "The Boulevard" meant Hollywood Boulevard, and the Red Velvet was a spot up on Wilcox run by my HPS classmate Sandy Ferra's dad, Tony Ferra.

I'd have preferred to spend some more time going over the script, but it was obvious that John Ashley was done being Constantin Stanislavsky. I owed him for recommending me for this part, and this was the least I could do to pay him back.

• • •

We pulled out of the Fountain Lanai's garage and up onto Sunset. I was still full of questions about the film. "John, listen, I know you're going to do okay on this, and I'm going to be making scale for the length of the shoot, but I'm looking at what it can mean for my career."

"This is the kind of movie that nobody who counts will ever see. It's a credit. But there's something else. This is being made in a small Midwestern town, with all the local extras who'll look like a million other Midwestern high-school kids. There's a pretty good car sequence in it—I mean, big deal—there's a car race in every teen-screener; it's part of the formula. But we'll be doing our own stunts. And if O'Dale directs this right, it'll be hairier than the one in *Rebel Without a Cause*."

"So, if nobody who counts ever sees it—how's that count?"

"Look, you've been in the biz long enough to know that it's all about bottom line. This shit-script piece of B-drek is going to run and run and run in every one of those little hick towns like Chillicothe, in every state between here and New York and Canada and Mexico. It's gonna be one hell of a grosser.

"So we play to those kids; we become those kids; we act like those kids act. And O'Dale will find another dog of a low-budge script, and we'll do another. But this time, you'll hold out for scale *and* points. And the guys who look only at the bottom line will say, 'The cast had something in that train wreck of a film; get 'em for ours.'"

Ashley was leaning against the door, pulling on a Camel. He wasn't the kind of actor who'd win an Oscar, but he was the kind of actor who'd never need to win an Oscar. He was handsome and smart. He'd always star in B's and eventually play supporting male roles in features. And he knew all the dangles and all the angles.

And he'd just taught me a strategy I could both understand and use.

25

ANOTHER DIMENSION

Pulling up at the light on Sunset and Wilcox, I reached for the pack of cigarettes that I'd put on the seat.

My hand encountered the cold steel and walnut stocks of Itchy's Smith & Wesson .32. I'd stuffed it into the crease in the Pontiac's seat. Under the overhead streetlight Ashley saw it at the same time.

"Oh, packing heat now, huh?"

Ashley had grown up in Oklahoma, and the sight of a pistol was nothing new, but I could tell by the look on his face that seeing me with a firearm was a surprise.

"Aw, no big deal, just a gift from a friend."

"No big deal in Oklahoma, but I don't know about here."

I smiled, gave a shrug, and pushed it under the waistband of my slacks.

Just before we reached the Red Velvet, two blondes started jaywalking across Wilcox, and I stopped before the intersection to let them pass. The frontal and profile views were impressive enough for both of us to fail to notice the car that had pulled up behind us.

As the girls reached the sidewalk and turned toward the club and line outside, Ashley made eye contact with the taller of the two, who was, even by Hollywood standards—gorgeous. He motioned for her to come over to the car, and to facilitate the delicate premating ritual, I U-ied across the street and pulled up to the curb.

WHOOP!

My hands froze on the wheel.

It was a half-second-long warning punch from the Los Angeles Police Department's black-and-white that had been behind us, now with red lights pulsing. I turned with my right arm over the seat and saw the officer motioning me to step out of the car.

Standing up and turning toward the officer who was getting out of the passenger's side of the patrol car, I reached in my back pocket for my wallet to produce my license as he came around the back of the Pontiac.

And the little S&W slipped from my waistband through my trouser leg, and clattered to the street at my feet.

Suddenly, I had entered another dimension.

The policeman's was a drilled reaction. Crouch, drop five-cell flashlight from shoulder position, draw service weapon, and assume two-handed Weaver stance. "FREEZE! HANDS UP WHERE I CAN SEE THEM!"

From the driver's side of the LAPD unit, the other officer was out, behind the door, pistol drawn, and shielded by the car's door.

"SIR, YOU IN THE PASSENGER SIDE OF THE VEHICLE, PUT YOUR LEFT HAND ON YOUR HEAD, OPEN THE DOOR SLOWLY, AND PUT YOUR RIGHT HAND ON YOUR HEAD— NOW!"

Ashley, wide-eyed, carefully and in what seemed to me almost slow motion, emerged from the car with his hands on top of his head.

"You, down! On the ground. Hands out!"

I felt his knee in my back, one hand jacked up behind me, heard the slapping mechanical sound of the handcuff's jaws closing, and then felt my other arm wrenched nearly from the socket, and cuffed. Standing now, he kicked my legs wide apart with his boot, and reached down and patted me down.

From the corner of my eye, looking under the car I could see Ashley, facedown on the passenger side, and the other officer's Wellington boots straddling him as he was cuffed and patted down.

Two more LAPD patrol cars pulled up, and by now we were the evening's main attraction. Examining my ID, which I'd had to painfully extract from my hip pocket with my right hand, the officer pulled me to my feet and handed my wallet to the sergeant who'd just arrived.

"All right, Mr. Stevens," he began. But before he could get the next words out of his mouth, a woman came pushing out of the crowd in a skirt that looked like an overstuffed lampshade and cried "See that guy! That one. The little guy, Officer! He was in the restaurant I work at the other night with Mickey Cohen!"

At the mention of the name Mickey Cohen, an immediate and adverse chemical reaction took place in the officer's physiology. It wasn't the first time I'd noticed this phenomenon, but it was the first time I'd been the direct object of such a response.

From standing, WHAM, I was back to a prone position, deposited by a swift sweep of the deputy's leg. No doubt a move learned in the academy and practiced with enthusiastic delight when protocol indicated.

Down again, this time with my mug in a wad of discarded chewing gum laced with a crushed cigarette butt, I had a moment to reflect before I was lifted bodily by two other officers and stuffed into the back of what looked to be the watch commander's vehicle. It was newer and shinier than the other units. Star treatment, no doubt.

Then the other back door opened, and a very apprehensive Johnny was shoved in beside me. "What the shi—" he started to say.

"I'll tell 'em you didn't know I had the gun," I managed to whisper before the other officer, climbing into the passenger seat, banged the cage screen with the baton he was removing so he could sit down.

"Shut up! You'll have a chance to get your stories straight later."

The sergeant I'd assumed was the WC climbed in, and the patrol car turned and headed back down Sunset.

Other-dimension consciousness.

Twenty minutes ago I'd been riding in my beautiful convertible down this street I knew so well—a free man. Now I was hunched forward with my hands cuffed behind me, knees under my chin. Going off into the night and a fate unknown.

I felt like a character dreamed up by Rod Serling.

Serling loved juxtapositional situations like this—*Man doing one thing suddenly finds himself, unwittingly or unwillingly, doing—or being forced to do—another.* These types of situations formed the core of his popular TV show and had become an iconic staple of America's viewing enjoyment.

But now I was in my own, carelessly engineered T-Zone.

I could hear Serling's sardonic, precisely pronounced words, spoken through an upward-drifting contrail of cigarette smoke.

"Here we meet a somewhat carefree young man who has become a victim of his own lack of clarity, his own failure to assume responsibility for a small metal object that bore more significance than weight, and would transform Steve Stevens, actor, into Prisoner Stevens, S. #00000 – 00000 and a long stay in the Twilight Zone."

26

NEWSBOY BLUES

W_{E PULLED INTO} the LAPD's Hollywood Division Station, a few blocks south on Wilcox and Homewood, and Ashley was immediately recognized by the booking officer, who had recently seen him in *Dragstrip Girl* and *The Cool and the Crazy*.

We were photographed, fingerprinted, asked to sign the inventories of our personal property, and led back to the holding area. Ashley still wasn't speaking to me, and it was easy to understand why.

Inside the "tank," at least some of our fellow miscreants were momentarily distracted by our entrance. One drunk quit vomiting long enough to look up, wipe his mouth, and sink to his knees. Two black men converged on me, asking if I had smokes. A big guy who had been showing amorous attention to a transvestite removed his hand from under his/her dress and looked carefully at Ashley—who was backed up against the steel mesh with his arms folded protectively over his chest.

"Ashley! You got your phone call," reported an officer who appeared with a ring of keys and unlocked the steel-mesh door.

I found a seat on the slightly-less-than-piss-damp cement floor between two sleeping drunks, made myself as small as possible, and began weighing my options.

I could call my father, but I wouldn't. There was no way. Waking him up, telling him I'd been booked on a concealed weapons charge was unthinkable. I'd stay in jail until whatever happened, happened. But causing him grief and embarrassment was not an option.

At the corridor's end I could see Ashley hanging up the telephone. A moment later another officer let him back in. He was clearly relieved.

"I just spoke with my attorney. He's on his way down. All you have to do is admit I didn't know anything about your pistol and there's no real problem—not even a court appearance."

Being a callow youth, my response was appropriately callow and youthfully inappropriate. "Well, next time you get a part, like, if you're in a jail scene, this'll come in really handy. You'll really be able to make it Method."

"Move over, dickhead." Ashley shook his head as he tried to sit down.

"Johnny, do you know where we are, man? This is the same police station they used in *Rebel Without a Cause*. How cool is that! James Dean sat right here in his red windbreaker, remember—"You're tearing me apart!" I yelled, summoning my vestigial reserves of teenage angst in my best Dean imitation.

Audience reaction was immediate. One of the sitting drunks fell over and began voiding his bladder, and a tattooed, eye-patched Cyclops arose from another part of the cell, fixed his one good bloodshot eye on us, recognized us for the sheep in wolf's clothing that we were—and swept aside the human debris that blocked his direct path.

"You—yeah you, cuntface—gimme a smoke 'fore I fuck you up!"

The basic human responses to danger are supposed to be

fight or flight, but what the hell do you do when fighting is senseless and flight is impossible? Withdraw into your inner zone of calming radiance?

Apparently not. Ashley was experiencing capillary vascular constriction—his face was turning white with fear.

I, on the other hand, reacted with recto-abdominal constriction—my stomach knotted up and my sphincter spasmed as I anticipated his size-13 biker boot planting itself on my dollar-earning countenance.

Easing to my feet, I began searching my pockets for an overlooked cigarette. Ashley remained frozen.

"Well, twat lips, you got it?" Cyclops threatened.

We both shook our heads in unison.

"Then I'm gonna have to relieve my nicotine craving by beating the living shit out of you cocksuckers."

"Hey, man, cool it." This from a young Mexican guy with a bandanna tied around his head.

"Get the fuck outta here, shit-taco."

"Be cool, I'm tellin' ju—the little guy is one a' Mickey Cohen's *familia*. Ju don' wanna mess with them, man."

Cyclops stepped back. Aggression drained from his face, revealing his otherwise ugly countenance. Something had obviously connected in his reptilian brain. An epiphany? Could it be the name Cohen, a member of the priestly tribe of Israel?

"Aw, shit, dude," said Cyclops. "I didn't mean nothin'. 'S'cool."

He offered his hand to Ashley to help him up and John accepted. I shook my head. *You play tuff guys real good.* And at that moment I played the tuffest guy I could conjure up.

"Asshole, you just saved yourself losing your other eye," I hissed.

"'S'cool, man. Just jailhousing you, man. Don't mean nuthin'."

Just then the officer appeared and jangled his keys. Everybody who could, looked up. "Ashley, your lawyer's here," he said, opening the door.

John turned to me. "You want me to have him bail you, too?"

"Nah, that's okay. Take off. I haven't made up my mind yet."

"Well, if you need anything," he said. "Y'know?"

I nodded and John stuck his hand out. We shook briefly and he stepped out.

I turned to the young Mexican kid. He looked familiar, but under all the stress, memory wasn't pulling him up.

"See, man, ju don' remember me, but I remember you. I'm Marcello's cousin, Miguel. Remember? I took care of your uncle Mr. Cohen's car."

"Whoa, sure. Hey, thanks."

"No, es nada. Don't sweat it. We gotta take care a' each other around here. How come you're in?"

"Concealed weapon. Actually, I pulled a U-turn in front of the cops. It fell outta my pants when I got outta the car."

"Shit," he said, offering a cigarette. "You'll get off. Those chump cops. In California, carrying a concealed gun's a misdemeanor. Now, if it was a big bowie knife, *that's* a felony."

Keys jangled again, and the officer appeared. "Stevens! Lawyer's here."

"Hey, Miguel, man. Appreciate the legal tip."

"See you aroun', man," said Miguel. "An' be more careful."

Waiting for me in a little room was a man in a suit who introduced himself as Jack Dahlstrum, one of Mickey's attorneys, and Abe Phillips, his bail bondsman.

"I haven't read your arrest report yet, but from what they tell me, I'm not unduly concerned. You'll be arraigned, but whether or not you'll stand trial remains to be seen. Mickey, however, wants to see you immediately. We'll have to get your car out of impound. How much money do you have?"

"Maybe five or ten bucks."

"Well, that won't be enough."

As we stepped out of the room, the watch commander came

up holding a movie-fan magazine in his big fist. On the open page was a photo feature showing Annette and me.

"Hey, my girl's a big fan of the Mickey Mouse Club. Can you autograph this for her?"

"Sure," I said, and noticed the look of amazement on the attorney's face. "What's her name?"

As we stepped out of the police station, Dahlstrum turned to me. "So, now, you're in entertainment? You're not just one of Mickey's . . . uh, acquaintances?"

I nodded, wondering from whom Mickey had heard—and marveled at just how fast he'd responded.

27

DISCIPLINE

IT WAS 11:15 by the time Dahlstrum handed over a check to release my car from the LAPD impound lot.

"Don't forget to stop by Mickey's on your way home," Dahlstrum cautioned, leaning on my door.

"I'm headed over there right now," I said. I felt dirty, wanted a shower, and sleep, but seeing Mickey—to thank him for getting me out—took priority.

Pulling up at 705 Barrington, I glanced at my watch. Nearly midnight. Mickey was a night owl, so I knew it wouldn't be too late, but I didn't want to ring the doorbell. Its chimes sounded like a Good Humor ice-cream truck—so I knocked. Phil Packer opened the door.

"Kid, Mickey's pissed at you, so play it cool, huh?"

I nodded. "I fucked up," I said as I walked past him into the living room.

Sitting on the couch was the comedian Red Skelton, surrounded by Mickey, Itchy, the guy I thought of as the Fat Man, and several women I didn't know. Skelton was obviously entertaining everyone with a story he was acting out. The guffaws and belly laughs lightened my mood.

Spotting me, Mickey stood up, excused himself, and took my arm and pointed down the hall leading toward one of the back bedrooms where the hall turned and we were out of sight of the guests.

Something should have warned me, telegraphed his intention, but somehow I didn't get the message.

Just outside the bedroom, Mickey reached with his right hand to open the door and then in a blurring motion spun on his right foot, and hooked me full in my face with his left. The blow was so sudden, so unexpected, that besides knocking me to my knees, it left me dazed and disoriented. The pain radiated along the sides of my cheekbones in pulsating waves. As I tried to turn my head, it went down through my spine like an electric shock, jangling the sciatic nerves in my thighs and legs.

Before I could respond, he'd put a knee in my chest, bumped me into the room, closed the door with his heel, grabbed the lapels of my jacket, and pulled me to my feet.

Blood was flowing out of my nose and into my mouth. He threw me against a wall, banging my head against the corner of a picture frame. My eyes were tearing—I could no longer see clearly—and I stumbled, falling to my hands and knees before him.

He grabbed me by the collar and shook me so hard I couldn't breathe. "You little shit, don't you go getting no goddamn blood on my new carpet," he hissed and threw a handkerchief at me. I held it to my face.

"You know what this is about? Huh?" He shook me again. "This is about you don't ever carry a gun, you simpleminded little fuck. You don't got the guts to use one anyways. You just leave it under the car seat for emergencies. Got that?"

I mumbled through the blood, tears, and mucus that I did.

"It was on the seat, Mickey. I stuck the damn thing in my waist, and when I got out to show the cop my license it fell out."

"Ha-ha, that's good," Mickey said, laughing. "Real good. You're still just a dumb little shit, Kid, but 'at's why I love ya. This was just to remind you to think about everything you do from now on. It's hard, but ya gotta learn. Got it? Now, let's get you cleaned up."

He put my arm over his shoulder and boosted me into the bathroom, grabbed a towel, ran cold water on it, and handed it to me. I started dabbing my face, and Mickey opened the medicine cabinet and pulled out some cotton and medicine bottles.

Like a fighter's ringside second, Mickey used a septic pencil to carefully dab my cut and swollen lip, had me tilt my head back, and stuffed some cotton up into the nostril that was bleeding. I was still dizzy, but I sat on the side of the bathtub and let him practice his thug first aid.

"Keep this wet towel on your face while I go get you some ice." He was back in a minute or two with an ice pack he'd put together with bar towels. In a few minutes more the bleeding stopped.

"So, what was this good news you told Phil about?" Mickey lifted my ice pack and smiled.

"I've got a pretty good part coming up in *Playhouse 90*."

"No shit? Yeah, that's a big hit show. I like it. When's it on?"

"They'll start shooting in about a week." I stopped to spit out some blood. "I'm not sure when it'll air."

"How about I throw a little party for you when it does, and we can all watch it?"

"Sure, Uncle Mickey," I croaked, fearful of saying anything that would anger him. I wanted to stand up and check the damage to my face, hoping it wouldn't be so bad that I'd be unfit for the part and replaced; but Mickey was standing at the bathroom sink with the water running.

"I'da known you were gonna do that, I'da hit you in the

gut," he said to his reflection in the mirror. "But you should be okay. You go out, have Phil make you a drink. Keep that ice on."

He turned and began his ritual handwashing.

I dreaded walking through the living room. Red Skelton was my favorite comedian, and I'd have enjoyed meeting him and listening to his stories. But not this way—looking like Mickey's punching bag.

And the worst thing? I was stupidly blaming myself—as if what I'd done merited his violent reaction.

I edged down the hall, melted water from the ice pack dripping on my shirt. Peeking around the corner I could see the living room. Only Phil Packer and the Fat Man were visible. Phil looked obliquely at me and headed for the bar, held up a bottle of Myers's rum and lifted his eyebrows. I nodded.

Fat Man stared at me the way he'd done a few weeks before. It was a predatory, rapacious look—like a vulture waiting for a lump of roadkill to stop twitching. And it angered me, made me feel even more vulnerable, more powerless. Phil must have sensed the mutual acrimony. He motioned me to the bar where he was washing glasses, and where I could sit with my back to the creep.

By the time I'd finished my drink, Mickey came back in.

"So where you living?" he asked.

"Fountain Lanai. I'm rooming with John Ashley, another actor."

"Oh, yeah, I heard you mention him. How long you lived there?"

"Not too long. He's been there for a couple of years."

"I got an idea. Why don't you bring Johnny over here for dinner tomorrow night? I wanna meet this movie-star pal of yours."

"Sure, Uncle Mickey, I'll ask him."

"You do that, ask him and call me—let me know if he can come. Now, get outta here and get some sleep. Ya look terrible."

Understandable, given you're a former professional welter-weight, I thought. Letting myself out the door, I took four steps and paused to clear my head. All I needed was another concussion after my long bout in the Navy Hospital in San Diego almost two years ago.

By now it was almost 2:00 a.m.

Taking my time—and watching red lights—I drove back to the Fountain Lanai. Letting myself into our apartment quietly, I could see the beast with two backs moving on the couch.

Fuckin' Ashley's fucking.

Somehow—between getting out of the Hollywood Division Police Station and this golden moment—he had found available sexual solace.

Somehow, I'd managed to have my criminal benefactor practice his good left hook on my best physical asset.

I turned the light on in my bathroom and moved in close to the mirror to do damage assessment. Damn. That was some door I'd walked into.

At least some of my luck was holding—he hadn't shot me.

28

MICKEY'S MONDO DINNER

THEY WERE FITTING the iron mask over my face. The pain was beyond intense as they closed it and the spikes drilled into my skin. It wouldn't quite close, so they started tapping it with a hammer . . .

Tap—tap—tap.

I gasped in agony. Tap—tap—tap.

"Steve-O, wake up, man. Let's go get some breakfast."

My eyes opened, sort of. I wasn't in the Bastille. The tapping was John Ashley—peering in my bedroom door.

I'd been sleeping on my stomach, facedown in my pillow. The pain had come from my two half-swollen-shut eyes and if-not-broken-damn-near nose. I sat up.

"Come in," I croaked.

"Jesus, what the—did that big guy in the jail—"

Just like Mickey and the flowers, Ashley had just given me the glory story I needed.

"He nailed me just as I was walking out."

"No shit. You got a puffy lip and a shiner. Will your pal Mick—"

"Nah. The Mexican kid saw it." I slid out of bed and leaned over my dresser's mirror with my back to John, relieved that the visual tissue damage was not as bad as the invisible ego trauma.

"He said he knows that guy and he'll take care of him," I lied. "Hey, speaking of Mickey, he invited you to join us for dinner at his place tonight."

Ashley looked at me as though I'd just handed him a poison toad. "Tonight? I—well—not tonight, I—"

"Look, John, this is not exactly the kind of opportunity guys like us get every day. Mickey isn't something out of a movie, he's the real thing."

"But he's a ga-ga . . . ," he stuttered.

"Gangster? Yeah. Maybe that's his job description, but he's a lot of other things, too, including a guy who when I told him about you really wanted to meet you. A couple of hours—man, it's nothing. You can be back here by ten getting laid. Besides, he's been running around a lot with Candy Barr; who knows, she might even be there."

• • •

Nobody used the term "denial" in those days of pre-pop psychology, but that's what it was—in its most severe form. I was not only completely ignoring the reality of the situation, I'd dissociated from it.

I couldn't admit, even to myself, that Mickey had done this—had beaten me. Almost immediately I'd substituted his rationalization—that he'd done this "for my own good," so I'd "pay attention"—for the blunt reality of his psychopathic behavior.

I'd witnessed his brutality before, and my reaction had been to romanticize it. Now, instead of reacting with justifiable indignation, resentment—hell, anything that would indicate I was reacting with some degree of insight into what he'd done, and how I'd responded—I was excusing his behavior.

It hadn't occurred to me at the time, nor did it occur to me the next morning, that something was seriously, self-destructively wrong with my behavior; that instead of running out of Mickey's apartment, instead of vowing never to see the bastard again, I'd agreed to have dinner with him tonight.

Then, instead of outrage when John saw and reacted to the results of Mickey's handiwork, I lied about who had done this to me, protected my attacker, excused his brutality, and further, in absolute denial—asked John to join us.

• • •

We arrived at Mickey's at seven thirty that night, and the door was opened by a buxom "maid" with thick blonde pigtails wearing a suspiciously minimal Hansel and Gretel outfit with a lace-up bodice that elevated her more-than-bountiful endowments to eye level and looked more like it had come from Western Costumes than Domestic Service Supply.

In the living room, seated on a large sofa, were Phil Packer, dressed in a suspiciously conservative blue suit and matching knit tie, and Candy Barr, who was—suspiciously—dressed.

"Boys"—Mickey gestured expansively—"this here's Miss Candy Barr, a real class-act dancer." Having previously encountered Miss Barr—bare—and in close proximity, I somehow vaguely recalled her dancing abilities.

Mickey seated us at the bar while Phil made drinks. Candy flirted, and Johnny's eyes glazed over. I did a quick mental demographic census: *two gangsters, two actors, and a stripper. Mondo surreal mangiari.*

Holding a tray, Gretel appeared.

"You vill haff zome, please." It was more a command than an invitation. Maybe if we didn't, there'd be some corrective measures taken. I didn't actually see a riding crop, but then I wasn't really looking. Because when she leaned over it was hard to tell whether Gretel was serving hors d'oeuvres, or hors d' mammaries.

MICKEY AND CANDY BARR.

With our appetites thusly stimulated, we could now enjoy a nice little Brentwood dinner party. Directed by Federico Fellini.

• • •

Dinner was very good, but the show was even better.

Gretel wove back and forth from the kitchen, serving like a Wagnerian Valkyrie on a mission from Beowulf's meade hall. Every time she passed by, I stifled the urge to yell, "ODIN!" like Kirk Douglas in *The Vikings*.

Phil, ever the loquacious conversationalist, said, "yeah,"

"uh-huh," and "that's right" six times. When Mickey wasn't talking about Mickey, John was talking about John, and looking at Candy.

Ashley's libido-induced primate mating ritual reaction to Candy—whose reputation as a stripper had been enhanced by a certain endearing 8-millimeter film, *Smart Alec,* which most of Hollywood had seen—was far more profound than his reaction to Mickey, whom most of Hollywood had only heard of and frankly would have been delighted never to have seen.

Helen of Troy had only launched a thousand ships. Candy Barr had launched enough latent postwar sexuality to jump-start the porno industry.

It was beginning to dawn on me that Mickey's love of publicity and celebrity, his enthusiastic collecting of entertainment personalities, was the closest thing he had to a hobby. Mickey clearly delighted in surrounding himself with famous people and beautiful, if somewhat infamous, women.

But the nature of his relationship with those women seemed a little ambiguous to me. Obviously these were not women you'd find on the guest speaker's roster at the Junior League. And whatever films they'd made weren't distributed through United Artists.

At first I thought Mickey was just like any other rich and powerful guy, like the typical producer who didn't have to rely on his good looks to attract gorgeous women and loved the fact that he could sleep with them and show them off as a sign of his power. But now I wasn't so sure. About the sleeping part— anyhow.

Conversation ranged across a series of important topics including class-act-dancer career paths and housing.

"Nah," said Candy between half-chewed mouthfuls, "I'm a Texas girl. I worked all over perfecting my act. I was strippin' for Jack Ruby at his Vegas Club before he got the Carousel Club, and then for Abe Weinstein and down in Dallas before I came to the Largo. But I like it here better, and I'm plannin' on stayin'."

"So, Johnny, tell me about this Fountain place you guys are living in."

"Fountain Lanai? I've been there a couple of years. It's a great spot, convenient to everything."

"You planning on moving, Mickey?" I asked.

"Nah, just looking for a new place 'at'd be good for Candy."

"There hasn't been a vacancy there in six months," John volunteered.

"Ah, a vacancy can be arranged. But never mind that, Johnny, the Kid here's been telling me about you're going places in your acting career and how many movies you made."

At the mention of "career," John Ashley and his libido rejoined the group, expanding his scope of focus from Candy's assets to his host's obvious interest and good cinematic taste.

"Well, I have been making a number of smaller films in the past two years, such as the one Steve and I will be making. But luckily, these tend to be far more financially than artistically successful."

Mickey—who understood "financially" no matter how you pronounced it—was listening intently.

"Do me a favor, stand over here," Mickey said, beckoning Ashley to stand by him. "Phil, Kid, whatcha think? Are we practically the same size?"

Phil and I both nodded. Candy giggled. "I didn't know better, I'd say you practically look like brothers."

Mickey laughed. "So, Johnny, you ever heard a' Ben Hecht?"

"Of course, Mickey. Ben Hecht's a major player in the industry."

"An' did you know he's interested in making a big movie, whaddaya call it—"

"A feature?" I provided.

"Yeah, yeah. A feature, a big Technicolor feature about me."

As I said it, I glanced at John, who was adjusting his posture, positioning his feet the way Mickey did when he stood, and placing his left hand against his chest in Mickey's characteristic gesture. I knew John well enough to know it wasn't something conscious, but one of those unconscious, reflexive moves that actors make when putting themselves into character.

Mickey, on the other hand, had straightened out of his boxer's left-shoulder-down-and forward posture, tilted his head slightly to the side, the way John did, lifting one eyebrow and half smiling—as unconsciously as John.

"Well, tell me, Mickey, is this an actual project; has there been any development money put into it?"

"Johnny, ya gotta know Hecht bought the rights to my story, he's got a writer working on it right now. All I gotta do's find someone I think can play me like I really am."

"Mickey, playing you—just as you really are—would be any good actor's dream role."

"So, Johnny, now, you, as a actor, how do you see that role—your playing me?"

John Ashley came back into his own body, stood aside from Mickey, made full eye contact, and pitched him.

"A sensitive, intelligent guy, unbroken by a childhood without privilege, out on the streets as a frightened youngster—having to learn and earn the hard way with only his wits and fists to see him through. He beats bum raps, dodges fatal bullets, has to see his family through the occasional set of jailhouse bars, but turns from crime into a distinguished career in film!"

I had a sudden flash—bowler hats, checked pants and jackets, little Charlie Chaplin canes, shuffle-stepping into the limelight together: *PLAYING TONIGHT ONLY: Ashley & Cohen— the Vaudeville Team It's a Crime to Watch!*

Mickey's absolute delight was infectious. These two were

feeding each other's egos like a couple of piranhas consuming each other's tails.

Candy was staring at Mickey and Johnny as though they were a couple of puffed-up strutting Ben Johnson–esque Elizabethan comedic characters with codpieces as big as their outsized egos. But as anyone who knows Hollywood knows, those are the guys who get all the action.

At ten thirty, Mickey walked us to the door with his arms around John's and my shoulders. "Say, Johnny, do me a favor, huh? Get me one a' them things, whatcha call them? With a picture—"

"You mean a résumé? Sure. I'll give it to Steve."

"And you, Kid," Mickey added, leering at me. "Next time some big palooka takes a swing, you remember—duck."

We both laughed, and in my car John leaned back and lit a cigarette.

"The guy's fantastic. What magnetism. I never met anyone like that. It's like we've been friends since another life. My high-school principal was scarier than he was."

"Pretty amazing, isn't he? Now you know why I wanted you to meet him."

"And to think that I hesitated—that I was dragging my feet. Christ, Steve-O, I really owe you one."

"Candy and you seemed to be, um, hitting it off."

"Jesus—have you ever seen those movies? Christ, I had a hard-on for a week. My God! She's fantastic."

No sooner were we in the apartment than John was on the phone to Nick Adams, who'd played the role of "Chick" in *Rebel Without a Cause,* and recently the *FBI Story,* telling him about having dinner at Mickey's.

"I'm not kidding, Nick. Public Enemy Number One! Yeah? Just a second; why don't you ask him, he's right here." He put his hand over the phone's mouthpiece.

"Hey, talk to Nick. He wants to meet him."

"Sure," I said, taking the phone. "Yeah, Nick, how's it going? Sure, I don't know why not. Yeah, yeah, no problem. He's a great guy."

29

RED-JACKET RACKET

CHRISTMAS AND NEW YEAR'S were over, but the press of obligations hadn't slacked off.

I was feeling boxed in. For several weeks it had been one event after another, either my family, friends, Mickey, or John, at parties, dinners, plays, nightclubs, a birthday party. I hadn't had a single night alone or any downtime.

My agent, Hy Sieger, had called that afternoon confirming my part in the big TV series *Gunsmoke* and had sent a script over. It was a good part, and I buried myself in trying to feel how I'd play it. Now I needed to get out, and a drink sounded like the right medicine.

Off Wilshire on Rodeo Drive in Beverly Hills was a Polynesian-style restaurant with a wonderful bar called the Luau that a lot of my buddies frequented. It was a great high-end low-profile spot, owned by Steve Crane, Lana Turner's former husband. Crane tolerated a few of us who had pretty good fake IDs.

Finding a parking spot a block away saved the valet tariff, and I walked the short distance, enjoying the clear, crisp January evening.

STEVE CRANE'S LUAU RESTAURANT.

Inside, the Luau looked like a set for a South Seas movie, huge lush green ferns and plants, illuminated aquariums full of exotic tropical fish, pandanus matting and tapa-cloth panels on the walls, an outrigger canoe hanging from the ceiling, and blowfish lamps.

It was a slow night, and the bar wasn't crowded at this hour. As my eyes adjusted to the soft amber light, I saw Marc Cavell, another Hollywood Professional School graduate who'd enlisted in the Marines with me, beckoning me to join him at the bar.

Marc was excited; he'd just started working on a new Allied Artists film, *The Purple Gang.* He had star billing next to Robert Blake, who played a psychopathic killer who leads a teenage Capone-era Chicago rat pack. It was a good script and would mean a big boost to Marc's career.

We caught up on our careers since the Marine Corps and on

our HPS schoolmates, who were now in their late teens and early twenties and beginning to make careers for themselves.

I told him about my roles in *Breaking Point* and *Mr. Novak*, where I'd played with James Franciscus and Dean Jagger, and my upcoming role as the supporting ingenue/acolyte to John Ashley's rich-kid gang leader in *High School Caesar*.

"So, speaking of gangsters, Steve, what's this about you hanging out with Mickey Cohen?" he asked. "I ran into Putnam and Lockwood the other night. They're worried about you."

"Aw, it's no big deal or anything. He likes actors and loves the nightlife. And believe me, he's nothing like the stuff you read about in the newspapers or see on TV. The guy's actually a lot of fun."

Getting up to leave, Cavell looked skeptical. "Well, watch your tail and flanks, Steve, and Semper Fi."

As Marc walked out, I glanced at two men who'd been sitting at the end of the bar and kept looking at me. They looked familiar, but I couldn't place them.

Mike, the bartender, leaned over and offered me a light. "Those guys want to buy you a drink," he said.

"Tell them thanks, but no thanks, Mike. I'm uncomfortable accepting drinks from people I don't know."

Mike relayed the message, and the larger of the two men stood up and walked over, taking the seat next to me.

"No disrespect intended, but aren't you an associate of Mr. Cohen's?"

Associate? said my little shoulder angel. *Is that what people are calling you now?*

"We was introduced a few weeks ago at the Apple Pan when you were eating with Mr. Cohen."

"Oh, yeah, of course." I was racking my brain, but so many people approached Mickey, no matter where he was, that the endless stream had begun blending into one indistinct mass of faces and extended hands.

His companion joined us, and it was clear from the way both were treating me that they were firmly convinced I was one of Mickey's wiseguys.

See? said the little white-winged nag. Then the little guy on the other shoulder with the pointed tail and the pitchfork chimed in. *Yeah, well, it's kinda cool, isn't it, you little harp-playing tattletale.*

"You guys come here often?" I asked. I'd never seen them before, and their dress and behavior were more downtown L.A. than Beverly Hills.

"Nah," said the smaller man, lowering his voice and looking around furtively. "We got some business."

Removing the requisite rum-drink umbrella, I took a sip of my new drink and said casually, "Yeah? So, Mickey knows about this?"

"Nah, that's why we're talkin' to you. Bizness bein' bizness. You can tell him—territory bein' territory and all—but we got this little deal with the maiter dee and two of the val-lays outside."

Their racket worked like this: The maître d' took a reservation, and alerted his two car parkers outside. When the marks entered the restaurant, they pulled the address off the car's registration. Figuring they would be there at least two hours, the maître d' called these two guys who drove over and burglarized the clueless victim's house. If it looked like the marks were leaving too soon, a tire would be flattened.

"Deal is, even with a five-way split, we make a ton a' dough. And tonight we got us a producer coming in. It'll be our biggest score of all."

"That's real good," I said, wondering just who their evening's mark would be. Jack Warner, maybe; or Darryl Zanuck? "Mickey'll be glad to talk to you about this, I'm sure." *And make it a six-way split,* I thought.

"The guy's named Nicholson. And he's due here any time."

What these two goons didn't know was that James H. Nicholson and his partner, Samuel Arkoff, were the heads of American International Pictures—the kings of B pictures. And, as luck would have it, their number one star was my roommate, John Ashley, who had invited me to Nicholson's house over Christmas for screenings.

Now's your chance to prove you're no gangster, said my little shoulder angel.

"Well, guys, thanks for the drink," I said, "but I gotta meet Mickey."

• • •

Outside I walked quickly to my car, trying to formulate a plan that would save Nicholson's house from these two scumbags. Whatever I came up with had to be cool. Neither of the car parkers had seen what I was driving, so I could count on my car being unrecognizable. A plus.

Calling the cops would be the easiest but the most dangerous option. They'd figure I was involved and it was some kind of sour-grapes rat-out. Besides, the cops already knew I was involved with Mickey, and that made me vulnerable to being turned into a snitch by threatening to tell Mickey that I was snitching.

If I told Mickey, he'd probably think it was a great idea and—being the area's crime boss—would no doubt want to be cut in. That would make me doubly complicit.

That left calling Nicholson and telling him. Nope. He'd want to know how I knew, and probably call the cops, who'd pick me up and cha-cha-cha.

That left two hours.

Whatever I was going to do would require doing it alone. I couldn't call a friend like Jock, because if anything screwballed, it would mean that I'd be bringing three-way heat down on me—and my hapless pal.

I'd played out a bad-buddy scene the other night with Ashley—with near-disastrous results. I wasn't going to expose anyone else to this. Screw that. I had to use my brain, and use it quick.

It would take twenty minutes to get to the Nicholsons' estate just off Mulholland Drive. That gave me some time to think. By the time I got there maybe I'd have something figured out. At least I'd beat those two idiots there, and what happened next would be pure improvisation.

I took a fresh pack of Parliaments out of the Pontiac's dash box and pulled the cellophane off with my teeth, rapped the top of the pack the requisite three times on the steering wheel, and worked out a smoke.

By the time I got there I'd chain-smoked four cigarettes, listened to local DJ Hunter Hancock playing requests, and cobbled together what passed for a half-assed plan.

Marine Corps doctrine was to attack with the element of surprise. I had the element of surprise all right, but I wasn't sure what to attack with. Then it dawned on me. *Headlights.*

I'd shine a little light on the cockroaches, and if that didn't do the trick, well, I'd tried.

Pulling past the Nicholsons' drive, I U-turned and slid my car under a large sycamore tree with low-hanging branches. I could see anyone coming from either behind me in the rearview mirror, or the more likely route—the way I'd come. I was hidden in a deep pool of shadow cast by the tree—smoking, watching, and listening to the radio.

"And now, for the number one request in the Southland, Hollywood's own Ricky Nelson's 'Lonesome Town.'"

Sitting there, pretending I was some half-assed solo gang-busting Galahad about to selflessly save the personal possessions of a rich—and no doubt well-insured—man whom I'd met just once, it suddenly dawned on me.

Here's Steve Stevens, listening to a chart-topper sung by Ricky Nelson, a personal friend, the current teen singing idol, a kid with a spotless career, who characterizes everything that is good and normal in American life—while Steve's life is taking some pretty weird turns.

Ricky and I had hung out for about a year after meeting at a party at his house. He'd invited my girlfriend at the time—another Hollywood Professional School student—Lorrie Collins, of the Collins Kids, a top country-and-western musical act.

I'd also appeared with Ricky on *The Adventures of Ozzie and Harriet*. Tonight he was playing a concert somewhere. The Nelsons had a beach house in Laguna, not far from Lockwood's family. Now I was hanging out—not with peers, actors, and entertainers—but with, as Ashley had put it the other night, "Public Enemy Number One."

And relying on my headlights.

It's a good thing I play tuff guys so well, I thought. *Otherwise, I might be scared shitless.*

Well, maybe they wouldn't show up.

Fat chance.

Coming toward me was a beat-up Chevy panel truck. Not the kind that makes deliveries in this neighborhood at night. And certainly not driving with the lights off. Pulling up just past the drive, they got out wearing stocking masks and black woolen watch caps.

Boy, I thought. *Burglars. Right out of Central Casting.*

I put my toe on the bright button and turned on the Pontiac's double headlamps.

ZAP!

Whoa! It worked. They tumbled back into the van and drove off. I waited, partly in fear of having them confront me at the end of the street where they might be waiting to see the car that had just surprised them.

So I sat, smoking and sweating nervously, and feeling a headache starting to pound to the rhythm of my elevated pulse rate.

And back they crept. Lights off, driving slowly.

Da cappo. I put my toe on the bright button and flashed on the Pontiac's double headlamps again—and they U-turned so fast they almost rolled the panel truck.

Suddenly the headache disappeared, the stale taste of one-too-many cigarettes was gone, and the warm glow of pulling off a clean little caper was erasing the residual fear. I felt good. James H. Nicholson would never know, never even suspect what I'd done. If he did, no doubt he'd have cast me in a few of his other movies.

But I knew. And my little shoulder angel kicked me in the earlobe.

Attaboy, Stevens. Good work.

30

DRUGSTORE BIG SHOT

"So, Kid, how's the actor business?"

"Bustin' tail and makin' scale, Uncle Mickey." It was good hearing Mickey's voice, and I found myself pleased that he was calling me. I'd been busy with a long shooting schedule for the TV show *The Breaking Point,* which had been stretched due to last-minute script changes.

"I love t' hear it. Ya got any time for your old uncle Mickey? Me and the boys are going over to have a little dessert at Schwab's in a while. If you can break away, you join us. What about Johnny?"

"He's out on a date," I said. And didn't mention that I thought it might be with Candy Barr. Ashley had been a little circumspect about just who he was seeing tonight, but from something he'd said a few days before, I had suspicions that he might be looking for a piece of Candy.

Schwab's Drugstore on Sunset Boulevard was a big hangout. It was only a few blocks away, and getting out, stretching my legs, and enjoying a low-key Friday walking up Crescent Heights to Sunset sounded good. I threw on a windbreaker and left.

The right side of Schwab's held the café and soda fountain. On the other side was the pharmacy, a large magazine rack, and a section that carried sundries and high-end cosmetics. Walking in, I saw big-name actors, little-name actors, no-name wannabes, an occasional director or agent, screenwriters, gossip columnists, PR flacks, and fan-mag hacks; it was a busy place full of people picking up prescriptions. Or if they weren't—taking an hour over a Coke or a cup of coffee—trying to look like they were.

Rafael Campos, a close friend and an actor who'd starred in *Blackboard Jungle* and *Trial,* was sitting in a booth with Sal Mineo, who'd just finished *Exodus* and hadn't been out of work since playing with James Dean in *Rebel Without a Cause.* He gestured for me to join them, and I slid in while he introduced me to Mineo.

"So who you here to see?" Rafael asked.

"Those guys over there," I said. "The ones that look like they're here to repossess the booths." I pointed to Mickey, Joe, and Fred.

Mickey, ever the apostle of anonymity, had positioned himself in one of the three booths that everyone in the place would have to either pass by or see—if they weren't on crutches or blind. Sid Skolsky was in one of the others—his regular one.

"You gotta be kidding. That's Mickey Cohen." Rafael wasn't speechless, but he looked somewhere between incredulous and astounded.

"Yeah," I said. "Skolsky hasn't been giving me enough ink. Thought I'd make sure he knew I existed. Come over in a few minutes; I'll introduce you."

Sidney Skolsky had never written a line about me; in fact, I doubt he even knew I existed. But one thing I'd noticed about hanging out with Mickey—whom everybody noticed—was that you *did* get noticed.

Sidney Skolsky used "his" booth at Schwab's as his informal second office, where he met people in the business and wrote about Hollywood. He'd had a long and successful career in film that included writing and producing *The Al Jolson Story,* writing *The Eddy Cantor Story,* and acting in such films as Billy Wilder's noir romance classic *Sunset Boulevard.* Skolsky remained as expressionless as a Gardena poker club regular. But he had taken notice. Comforting.

Maybe I'd "arrived." Or, short of that, maybe I'd achieved "Schwab's Celebrity" status. Not quite as good as "arrived," but at least Mickey didn't hold that against me.

"Well, look who's finally made it through the crowd—the guy who knows everybody. Hey, Kid, you see that guy over there? He's from my side a' the street. He's the only real hard-time ex-con you see up on the screen. Hey, Leo!"

Leo V. Gordon was a big, thickset, scary-looking character actor with a past more checkered than the tablecloths at Michelli's. He'd been shot, and he'd served a long sentence at San Quentin for stickups and strong-arm robberies before turning his life around. His black-hat roles in *Hondo, Cheyenne, Black Patch, Riot in Cell Block 11,* and in more than a dozen other films and on TV shows like *Colt .45, Bonanza,* and *Maverick* had garnered him a cult following among Hollywood's cognoscenti.

"Mickey, you old bastard, what the hell ya doing, casing this pansy patch for a knock-over?" Gordon's deep, menacing voice was a match for his physical presence.

Mickey and the Sicas all laughed. "Leo, the only thing in here worth stealing's your wise ass. I could always use another guy for my greenhouse crew."

"Greenhouse? Mickey, I turned over a new leaf," Leo pulled on his jacket's lapel. "See? Underneath's my probation officer."

Rafael walked up as Leo left, and I introduced him. Mickey had seen *Blackboard Jungle,* and he complimented Rafael on what a fine job he'd done. Rafael thanked him and, practically in the same breath, excused himself, saying he had an early call on the new TV show *Death Valley Days* he was working on with Ronald Reagan.

"Yeah, well, we got a late call on this project we been working on." Mickey grinned. "We'll be taking off, too."

I stood up and walked a few steps with Rafael while Mickey and the Sicas were getting out of the booth.

"Sure glad he liked my acting," Rafael said under his breath as he punched my shoulder. "What'n'hell would he have done if he hadn't?"

"Probably not much; he didn't bring his tommy gun tonight."

Mickey and the Sicas caught up with us, and we all passed Sid Skolsky's booth. This time Skolsky not only looked up, he nodded.

I couldn't resist my next move.

I gave Skolsky a big smile, and a wink.

31

MICKEY'S REMOTE CONTROL

JOHN ASHLEY AND I flew into Kansas City on a Saturday.

We were picked up by a local driver who'd been sent for us and were driven some ninety miles over the border to Chillicothe, Missouri, a tidy little Midwestern town built around a town square with a population of ten thousand. It had been O'Dale Ireland's boyhood home, and he'd no doubt chosen it with an eye toward picking up the feeling of America's Midwest.

We joined the rest of the cast and crew, who were staying in the Strand Hotel, the town's only hotel large enough to accommodate the group, and as actors do, we caught up on who'd been doing what films or shows and with whom.

Gary Vinson and Judy Nugent were old friends from previous TV and film work. Daria Massey, whom I'd met in O'Dale's office some months before, was every bit as sexy as I'd remembered—and it wasn't wasted on Ashley, who zeroed right in. I didn't know Lowell Brown, who played Kelly, and my first impression was that he seemed standoffish.

We were introduced to the local cast and went over some of the technical aspects that directors like to hash out before shooting starts. Since many scenes are nonsequential and require wardrobe changes and lighting and sound adjustments—especially a low-budget movie such as this one with little room for error—a lot of coordination takes place.

One of the strange coincidences I noticed was that the car John Ashley's character, Matt, was going to be driving in the movie was a 1958 Cadillac four-door hardtop convertible. Almost the same model Mickey drove.

That night Ashley and I—out for a smoke and a stroll around the town square—found ourselves witnessing an unusual local event. Young women from the state women's correctional facility were bused in and led as a group to the town's main theater to see the show. Standing on the curbs, leaning against parked cars and pickups, local guys were enjoying the parade. One guy, wearing Levi's, cowboy boots, and a white T-shirt with his cigarettes tucked up in one sleeve, gave a long wolf-whistle.

"You keep it in yo' pants for me, honey," one girl called out. "I'll only be another six months."

• • •

Our first day's shooting was scheduled for several locations in open country outside Chillicothe. When the Hollywood cast arrived, we were greeted by a crowd of several hundred interested local kids and adults, anxious to see how a real Hollywood movie was actually filmed.

Chillicothe's police department provided security, but when we'd finished shooting, O'Dale nodded and about a dozen local kids bolted toward us. Ashley nodded to me as the kids came swarming up. He was an old hand at autographs and teen-adulation. But instead of Johnny being mobbed, the kids ganged up around me. The "Annette" series was rerunning, and Chillicothe's newspaper, the *Constitution Tribune,* had picked up on it and written an article, complete with photos.

"Steve-O, it's your moment of fame; knock yourself out." John chuckled. But his chuckle was tinged with a little embarrassment. Where were his fans?

"Judy," I yelled to Miss Nugent, "c'mon over here and help me." The kids, of course, immediately recognized Judy as the "Jet" on the "Annette" series, and together we signed autographs and took pictures for the excited fans. What amazed us was just how popular the *Mickey Mouse Club* and "Annette" series were.

Off to one side, Johnny was centering his attention on Daria Massey, and it was apparently going a long way toward making up for his sudden loss of fan support. Daria could make just about any man forget just about anything for just about any length of time.

For a moment I envied him, but then the idea of giving up even a momentary dose of hungered-for star treatment for what might or might not result in a possible sexual moment was dismissed. I'd had sex before, but not much star treatment.

Back at the hotel, moment of fame and ego-adulation over and sitting down to dinner with Johnny, I looked up to see two guys approaching. They looked like they'd just stepped out of the 1950 Mafia stylebook. Wide-brimmed hats, obviously tailored but basically ugly suits, shirts and ties, cigars, and one with enough displayed jewelry to fill a pawnshop window. Rodgers and Hammerstein notwithstanding, I guess everything *wasn't* that up to date in Kansas City.

"Hey, which wunna yew is Steve Stevens?" They might dress New York, but their accents were local.

I looked up with my best boyishly ingratiating grin. "You promise not to break my kneecaps if I tell?" I goofed. John looked as if he were going to choke.

"No offense; we din't mean to innerup your meal, but could we have a word in private?"

"Only if you swear not to tell the director I was eating this meat loaf. He worries about my diet."

Looking at the plain, basic Midwestern food on our plates, this drew a joint chuckle from them.

Taking that as a good omen, I followed them into the lobby—noticing that the entire cast, crew, and recently attached hangers-on were wide-eyed with wonder. Probably at the jewelry.

By the lobby fireplace the bigger of the two men extended his hand. "I'm Angie Manggino."

"Yeah, we call him 'the Nose,'" the other man said.

"Yeah, you'll never guess why. And this here's Ritchie Di Santo, and his nickname's 'Sparkle Plenty,' as you can see. So, Mr. Cohen called an' asked if we could look out for his favorite actors."

"Nose" Manggino's nose was something worthy of Mount Rushmore, and Ritchie "Sparkle Plenty" Di Santo was bedecked with a diamond stickpin as big as a muscat grape, pinky-ring diamonds the size of jawbreakers, and a large ring mounting a piece of ice the size of a small glacier.

"Would that 'looking out' include a decent meal?"

"You bet. Mr. Cohen said to show you a good time in K.C."

"All right if I take my buddy in there? He's the star."

"Take him? We'll drag him kickin' 'n' screamin'." Angie guffawed.

"You watch out," I said, laughing. "If he smells pussy, he'll be dragging you."

"Sure. Whatever. We'll come back and pick you both up here. We just wanted to welcome ya."

They left trailing a cloud of very good-smelling cigar smoke.

Rejoining Ashley at the table, I could see that he was really concerned. "What happened? Are you okay? What did they want—"

"Johnny, cool out. They were sent by Uncle Mickey. He wants them to take us out on the town in Kansas City."

"Jesus! They looked like they stepped out of a George Raft movie. I didn't know what to think. I mean"—he paused and looked around—"you think they're safe?"

"Safe? Johnny, I think Mickey's just taking care of the guy who's gonna play him in his big movie."

32

"KANSAS CITY, HERE I COME"

THE DAY'S SHOOTING had been successful.

O'Dale was pleased, the cast was pleased, and Johnny was so sure we'd have a hit that he managed to hit on Daria three times with no success.

I was tired but anticipating a change of scenery. Cultural acclimatization to Chillicothe was proving psychologically and gastronomically challenging. I was a young man bred on a healthy portion of exciting Hollywood restaurants with inventive chefs, infinitely varied menus, and great bars.

As we'd discovered the night before, Chillicothe was somewhat more limited. Hamburger-based entrées were a culinary favorite. Falstaff beer seemed to be the regional beverage.

We were getting out of our wardrobe when a big black Lincoln pulled up. It had to be Sparkle Plenty and the Nose. People in Chillicothe didn't seem to drive cars like that.

I motioned. "Take a look, Johnny. Our chaperones." Joining Nose and Sparkle Plenty was a bigger, younger man with leading man's features.

"Hey, Steve. This here's Nicky; he wanted ta see what makin' a movie looked like. We din't wanna get underfoot, so we watched from a ways back."

"Good ta meet ya." Nick shook hands warmly. His accent was pure Chicago. "Mr. Ashley, I seen all your flicks. Every one. I loved *Dragstrip Girl, Suicide Battalion,* and *Zero Hour*—terrific. But I gotta be truthful, Steve. I never seen the *Mickey Mouse Club* . . . but I seen Annette. Holy mother. What a little dreamboat she is. And I'm ever out to Hollywood, you gotta introduce me."

I laughed. "You ever get to Hollywood, I'll put you right at the head of the line."

This got a laugh from everybody.

"You know, also I met your uncle Mickey. He's a terrific guy."

"Then you know how Uncle Mickey likes to take lots of showers, right? Well, it runs in the family. We need to get back to the hotel and wash off the makeup. Otherwise, the local guys'll get the wrong idea."

We piled into the big Lincoln and bounced over the country roads back to the hotel.

• • •

Speeding along at a steady seventy-five miles an hour, we covered the distance from Chillicothe to Kansas City, Kansas, in well under the two hours it had taken us to get to Chillicothe a few days before. Ashley kept the three men enraptured with his nonstop monologue.

"You guys know that I was born right here, Kansas City, Missouri? That's right. On Christmas Day. Thank God we're going across the river. Too many churches on the Missouri side."

They explained to me the difference between the staid, stodgy Missouri side of the city and the wide-open, anything-goes Kansas side.

"Now," said Nose, "you go to a strip joint on the Missouri side, the strippers is all Baptists and Methodists."

"Yeah," added Sparkle Plenty, "but over here, whoopee. They're all naked."

"And where we're takin' you for dinner," said Nicky, "the best steaks, the best seafood flown up fresh every day from New Orleans. And their desserts? Just like in New York, to die for."

"Die? Hey, aren't you guys here to protect us? We gotta finish this film," I joked.

"Yeah," said Ashley, "no dying. It'd ruin my career."

"Only thing we can't protect you from's your bad habits." Nick laughed. "And I hear we gotta few of those to cover, huh?"

"So he's hoping you brought all of them with you." Nose tapped his shoulder.

We'd pulled onto a narrow side street where Caddies, Chryslers, Lincolns, and Thunderbirds lined the curbs. We stopped in front of what appeared to be nothing more than a simple, unpretentious storefront. The windows were frosted, and only a small neon sign blinked on and off. As we approached, the door opened and a man in a tux, whom everyone seemed to know, ushered us inside.

"Maxi," said Nose, "this here's our special guests, Steve, Mr. Cohen's nephew, and Johnny. They're actors from Hollywood makin' a movie up in Chillicothe."

Maxi looked impressed. "You boys hungry?" We nodded. "Okay. We'll take good care of ya."

Inside, the place was larger than it had appeared from the outside, and it was obvious that the simplicity of the exterior belied the elegance and taste of the interior.

Drinks arrived and never stopped. Hush puppies and meat loaf didn't appear on the menu. Appetizers of chilled clams, shrimp, and oysters were served, and the three big men, all larger by a good fifty or sixty pounds than John or I, dug in.

Both John and I—with our last meal having been a box

lunch featuring unidentifiable processed luncheon meat on slightly stale white bread with wilted lettuce—kept up with the crowd. The steaks that followed were the stuff of Kansas City legend. John managed between mouthfuls to recount his film career in detail an archivist would have been proud of.

Maxi came over and directed the busboy to clear the table. "Now Mr. Manggino says you boys got a sweet tooth. So we're bringin' ya the house's special dessert."

Up came a wheeled cart with an elaborate silver serving dish, which Maxi then proceeded to turn into a flaming monstrosity with a gold Dunhill cigarette lighter.

I gasped. "Angie, I see what you mean about this dessert being to die for. If it doesn't give you third-degree burns, it'll kill you with diabetes."

"Aw, put it out with this, compliments of Maxi," Nicky said, pouring me a glass of Piper-Heidsieck champagne from a chilled magnum.

• • •

Nothing edible was left; all glasses and bottles were drained. Nicky was spellbound. The Nose nodded sagely. Sparkle Plenty sparkled plentifully as I entertained them with tales of Mickey Cohen, Annette, and Mickey Mouse.

"Steve, now I know you're probably older than you look, but what's with this *Mickey Mouse* thing? You really do that?"

"Look, the acting racket's just like any other racket. Everything's about entertainment whatever side you're working, right? You got an audience that wants a certain kind of entertainment, say, gambling, hookers, numbers, whatever. Just like you guys, we have bosses that run the entertainment racket— they hire guys and dolls—actors—to supply that need. The bosses take care of organizing things, the guys and dolls make their share doing their work, and the customers get their entertainment."

"So the *Mickey Mouse* thing's a racket? A scam?" Nose was curious. "You make up some fake shit and they buy it?"

"Just like that, but there's a little difference. It's for kids, and it keeps them happy. So it's the best racket there is. The kids love it, and we love them for loving it. Life's hard. We all know that. Who doesn't want to make kids happy?"

Nose Manggino looked at me and nodded. "A'course. Sure. I got nieces and nephews. Sparkle's got kids, don't you Sparkle?"

"Yeah, but I ain't seen them in a while cuza the divorce. They're in Cleveland. They like all that Mickey Mouse stuff."

"And because we gotta get up early and do our gig, we're gonna have to get back pretty soon," I said.

"We got a little business to take care a' first. Nicky's gonna take you around the corner to a little club. A little nightcap, huh? We'll pick you up soon's we're done."

We followed Nicky a few yards down the block and turned the corner. A neon marquee outside announced it was the Palm Room, a fact confirmed by a potted plant in what passed for the lobby/entrance. The bouncer, who looked like an unemployed gorilla, tipped his dusty top hat to Nicky, and we walked in.

Through the haze of cigarette smoke, the Palm Room revealed itself as a sleaze joint's classic sleaze joint. A few tables with customers, a bar, a stage in the corner of the room. And a stripper, grinding out the last bars of the current Tijuana Brass hit, "The Stripper."

Johnny was instantly enchanted.

And the three waitresses who descended on us like fruit bats on ripe mangoes were perfect. Nicky was obviously the man of the hour here, and no sooner had he taken a seat than the most attractive of the three was suddenly busy adjusting his minute hand.

Like magic, the other two flitted to the bar and returned with not only a tray full of whatever it was we'd ordered, but a real vampire.

Somebody had plumbed the innermost depths of my darkest, most prurient fantasies.

She was tall beyond the top of her four-inch spike heels. Her skin was a dead milky white. Her hair was jet black, cut in a bob with bangs. Her eyebrows were perfect dark crescents. She had a black beauty mark on her cheek. Her Clara Bow lips were outlined in a deep crimson lipstick the color of blood. Her dress was black taffeta, silk and black lace, and moved against her body like a black panther's skin.

She leaned over me, and her lace scarf descended on me like a black cloud. Under this she leaned forward, and her sharp teeth nipped my neck. It felt like an electrical shock.

"I'm Vampirella, and you are mine."

Undulating herself into the booth next to me, she eased her short black dress up over the black stockings and garter belt, making sure I could see her marble-white thighs and black lace panties. Her other hand fluttered across my stomach and hips. I was barely able to control my gut-contracting reflex.

Onstage the stripper took a round of applause, bent over—rear to the audience to collect and perhaps attract a few more scattered donations—and flounced offstage as the next act came on.

"You're tumescent," Vampirella said, unzipping my fly and easing her hands around me.

"Huh?" I mumbled.

"Your member is engorged with blood." Both her hands surrounded said member. "Vampires crave fresh blood, my little victim. I'm going to suck every drop from you. Then, you'll be one of us. Live forever, eternal damnation and pleasure, wrapped in the cloak of death . . ."

"All that," I gasped, "from little Monster down there—"

Vampirella's hands were moving with an interesting flexing motion. Nicky and Johnny had somehow evaporated.

"And now, Kansas City's darling, Baby Doll . . . ," an invisible emcee announced.

Another stripper was undoing her sleepers and diaper to reveal a lacy teddy, sucking lasciviously on a pacifier, and using a baby rattle in a way that Sigmund Freud would have found significant.

Nicky appeared out of the smoke.

"Hey, Steve-O, lookit me for a second. You need us, we're in the dressing room, backstage."

I'm sure I made some response, but by this time I was drooling, so it was probably indistinct.

My pants had somehow slipped down around my knees, and I was pushing back against the booth so hard I was probably terminally stressing the Naugahyde. Vampirella suddenly slipped beneath the table's horizon and began the process she'd so graphically described.

Did I call the Red Cross? Could I remember my blood type? How many units would a replacement transfusion require? I knew my brain had collapsed from the vacuum caused by suction, so I was probably thinking with only my other head.

Vampirella surfaced, smiled, produced a dainty hanky from her purse, and made certain skillful movements. "I—I—n-n-need a drink," I sputtered. "Where are the—"

She put a fresh drink in my hand, and I put it to use. "There may be more," she whispered. "You're not quite dead yet, are you? I think my little creature still has enough blood in him to survive another deadly encounter, hmmm? Follow me."

Being at least brain-dead if not quite dead-dead, and knowing that sacrifice was the sincerest form of something or other, I followed her wraithlike shadow down a corridor leading surely to hell, but stopping by a black door with a faded sequined star hanging slightly askew.

Vampirella tapped with her black inch-long nails, and Nick opened the door. Johnny was on his back on a dressing table, with one of the waitresses—relieved of her duty and uniform—planted squarely on his face, while the first stripper we'd seen was facing her—stripped—and securely seated on Johnny's mid-abdominal region, carefully guarding his private parts from unannounced inspection. He was obviously adequately covered and, with the compounded body warmth, wouldn't catch cold. Certain rhythmic motions and vocalizations indicated at least some level of consciousness.

Nicky, I noticed as he closed the door, had another of the waitresses on her knees and attached to his fly—probably making adjustments to a stuck zipper or inspecting garment construction. All of which had the astounding effect of creating another rush of blood to my drained appendage.

Like Jerry Lewis walking in on Dean Martin *in flagrante delicto,* I made a bumbling little wave and backed out of the room into Vampirella's arms. She turned me around and backed herself against the wall, lifting her dress and exposing her hips, thighs, and, gasp of erotic delight, the fatal garter belt.

Then she turned and I stood transfixed, watching those white hands with the black nails pulling at the panties beneath the heart-stopping garter belt.

Scandalous, but effective.

With the thumping sounds of Big Joe Turner's classic "Kansas City Here I Come" in the background, I stumbled somewhat drunkenly into action, saved by youth's vigor from leaving Vampirella's needs unfulfilled—but never quite remembering exactly what happened from that last flash of black lace and nylon and white cheeks, to waking up in the Lincoln at 0600 hours the next day, with our first call only an hour away.

That vampire was right. I'd died. And this—such as it was—was my afterlife.

And while the Hotel Strand's parking lot, though slightly surreal, wasn't exactly hell—my horrible hangover wasn't exactly heaven, either.

33

CRITICAL MASS

"Mr. Stevens? There's a long-distance call for you." The Strand's manager was waving me over.

"Take it over there if you'd like," he said, pointing across the lobby.

I separated from the rest of the crew and went to the little alcove with a marble counter and picked up the old-fashioned two-part telephone.

"Steve? I know you're very busy, but I have to speak with you."

Dad's voice had an edge of stress I'd never heard before.

He was a man who'd survived a lot—a tough childhood, the Great Depression, the war—but what he was describing to me over the phone, two thousand miles away in Chillicothe, was something neither of us had the knowledge or experience to fully grasp or deal with.

"Steve, your mother's taken a turn for the worse. The new medications we'd hoped would help her don't seem to be working. She's going into states—well, Dr. Cole calls it schizophrenia. She wanders off, physically, mentally; she gets withdrawn and then comes out swinging. We can't really seem to even communicate with her anymore. It's affecting your brother, and I'm at my wit's end. The doctor's saying we're going to have to consider institutionalization."

My knowledge of such things, like most people at that time, was limited. One definition, "crazy," fit all mental illnesses. And "crazy" carried with it the dual emotional burdens of shame and fear—shame that my mother was now essentially a social outcast, for that's what "crazy" people were and had been for countless generations of human ignorance and superstition—and fear that perhaps, because it was my mother, I might also be affected with something contagious, something nobody could understand or cure, and that seemed to have come like a curse from nowhere.

"Isn't there anything we can do; another doctor?" It was the cry of helplessness that anyone who's had a close family member or friend beset by this strange disorder has voiced. And for which there is never an adequate answer.

What my father had been discovering, and I was just learning, was that for all of modern medicine's huge advances in the mid-twentieth century, there was no penicillin, no effective medical treatment, for a mental illness like schizophrenia. Often the available treatments, electroshock and drugs such as Thorazine, had devastating zombielike effects on patients.

"Dad, listen," I told him. "I have a few more days on location, and I'll come back and help in any way I can. Jock Putnam's dad's the best neurosurgeon in Beverly Hills. Maybe he can tell us something or recommend another doctor."

At twenty, some people are more mature than others, and while I had a superficial level of sophistication, a mixture of real-world and Hollywood experience, seasoned with a dose of functional cynicism, I didn't have the emotional maturity to understand or foresee my reactions to what amounted to the slow loss of a parent. Nor had I developed the academic skills to access the available psychiatric educational resources that would provide enough insight to be able to truly assist.

Being helpless and struggling under the burden of guilt that my helplessness created also meant being unaware that my own psychological health was being impacted. It hadn't occurred to me that I could help myself, my father, my brother, and even my mother by seeking counseling. The whole concept—had I even thought of it—was too foreign. Tuff guys didn't need that shit. Tuff guys saved their own, solved their own problems, and never took no for an answer.

Subconsciously I fell back on what I knew, the film images I'd built my career on. Gregory Peck, grim, determined, implacable; Jimmy Stewart, sensitive but strong; Henry Fonda, troubled but effective. Once I found the right role, the right character, I'd go back and make things better, stand shoulder-to-shoulder with my father, encourage and support my brother, and somehow—with kryptonite, with a silver bullet, with the right combination of strength, love, and screenwritten Lone Ranger determination—save my mother.

Right now, standing in the Strand's lobby, with people milling around me and my father's desperation still echoing in my ears, I was James Dean in *East of Eden*.

Troubled by the news of a family catastrophe the Young Man sets the telephone earpiece back in its fork. Both hands go to his temples. He tries to contain the powerful wave of emotion that seeks to burst through the walls of his skull.

John Ashley approached me. "Hey, Steve, man. You okay?"

But the troubled Young Man pulls away. His angst, his trepidation, his pain must be born alone. His is a lonesome journey.

"Nah, just some bad news 'bout my mom. I need to be alone."

• • •

After making my exit I went to my room and lay down. I smoked more cigarettes. And then the burden of that aloneness weighed on me; I desperately wanted companionship, other people around me, anything to sidestep the grief that being alone amplifies.

Finding some of the cast in the hotel's bar, I smoked more cigarettes and drank. A headline on an article in a newspaper left on the barstool next to me read "World's Atomic Stockpiles Reaching Critical Mass." A scientist was claiming that with all the fissionable material available to the Soviets and Americans, under certain conditions a "critical mass" could be created and result in a nuclear chain reaction.

I reread the phrase. *Critical Mass.* It seemed like a metaphor for my life right now.

On one hand my career was really beginning to take off, sustaining itself with exciting parts with real potential. But my personal life seemed chaotic, pulled by conflicting positive and negative sources. And the anguish in my father's voice seemed to be pushing me to a kind of "critical mass." I had to do something, take effective action, before some chain reaction of events I couldn't foresee was set into motion.

• • •

O'Dale had scheduled shooting the film's last scene that night. In it, a deeply troubled Matt, Johnny's character, who was responsible for more tragedy than a small Midwestern high-school principal and a local hamburger joint's owner should be forced to bear, is finally abandoned by his own gang and his friends, and shunned by the rest. He falls to the ground in front of the town's hamburger hangout, in a fetal crouch, wailing in loneliness and pain.

During the last take, in one of those strange coincidences that have become the coin of Hollywood legend, a sudden little cyclonic wind descended from nowhere on John.

So powerful was the sudden effect on the whole scene that O'Dale shouted to the cameraman and light crew, "This is great; keep filming!"

Leaves and dust swirled around John and spiraled upward in the spotlight that pinned him to the ground.

Blowing his lines away.

I wrapped up a short retake of an earlier scene the next morning and flew home alone.

34

LABEL CAPER

DR. KAPLAN ANSWERED my questions patiently.

"No," he said, gesturing with his hands, "the range of effective medications available in your mother's case, such as Haldol and Thorazine, are limited. She is simply not responding well to them. Electroconvulsive therapy—the common term is 'shock treatment'—isn't indicated at this point, and I'm less than enthusiastic about it, in any case. As a treatment modality, my observations are that it is too potentially physically debilitating."

"What's it do?"

He used unfamiliar words like invasive, disorienting, and terms such as "neural transmitters," "verbal ability impairment," and "cortical damage." It didn't sound good.

"Our main concern at this juncture is to keep her from injuring herself. Schizophrenia is associated with a great deal of physically self-destructive behavior. Obviously, she'll need hospitalization for additional psychiatric evaluation, and then a stable environment and mild sedation to keep her periods of agitation limited."

"What kind of stable environment?" I asked.

My father had heard much of this before, and he tapped my arm. "My medical insurance doesn't cover mental disorders," he said softly. "It means Camarillo."

I looked sharply at him. "That place up by Oxnard? For Mom? That's where they put Charlie Parker."

"Camarillo Sate Mental Hospital," said the doctor. "It's one of the newer state institutions, built in the mid-thirties, in a very nice setting. But of course, it is an institution, and 'nice' is a relative term. As to Charlie Parker, the famous jazz alto sax man, he was a heroin addict, and I understand there was some success related to his treatment."

As we left Dr. Kaplan's Westwood office, my father explained he had already incurred a number of medical bills. With my brother, Reggie, still in high school, and Dad antici-pating the expenses of his upcoming four years at the University of Southern California, I did the only thing I could do. I gave him all the money I'd made on *High School Caesar*. It would also cover some of the additional expenses involved with the last-ditch efforts and third and fourth opinions.

That left me financially where I'd been earlier in the year.

My car payment was covered, my rent taken care of for two more months, but an actor's appearance is not only important, it's critical. And my hair needed cutting every ten days.

Al's Barber Shop, across from Schwab's on the corner of Crescent Heights and Sunset, was my usual spot. Al Martinez was leading-man good-looking, and he knew how to cut hair in a variety of Hollywood styles, calling mine his "Tony Curtis Cut."

This was a time when the term "hairstylist" wasn't in a man's lexicon, and no man I knew would ever have gone into a women's beauty salon. But there were several very respected and in-demand entertainment industry barbers in Hollywood and Beverly Hills, such as Jay Sebring.

One of these was in the little three-chair shop tucked in the back of Sy Devore's Men's Store, on Vine Street right across from the Brown Derby. Earlier I'd visited this spot with Ricky Nelson while he was having his hair trimmed, and come away impressed. I'd never imagined paying ten dollars for a haircut, but while I was waiting for Ricky and trying on

THE TONY CURTIS HAIRCUT.

clothing in Sy Devore's shop, an idea began formulating in my mind.

Sy Devore's clothing was a Hollywood phenomenon. He was enjoying a vogue as tailor to the stars. And if you could afford his outrageous prices, Devore's was where you went.

Since I preferred the very traditional, preppy look, Devore's flamboyantly styled and typically heavily padded garments were not something I even liked. But—perception being everything in Hollywood—I knew the value of having friends and enemies alike think you were wearing a Sy Devore jacket or slacks. It meant you were "working."

The next day—with my little shoulder angel going nuts on one shoulder and the little devil unable to contain his delight on the other—I went back with a Pal single-edge razorblade tucked into my wallet wrapped in the little cardboard sleeve that it came in. For a skilled craftsman, the correct tools are important.

I took three jackets into the changing room, went through the charade of trying them on and coming out to look in the mirror, and then returning—and with my razorblade removed two of the jackets' labels, which were sewn in by hand with an easily removed little chain stitch.

It was easy to walk into Schwab's two hours later and pick the types who might want such a rare item—and within another hour I'd sold both labels.

Needing a haircut, I headed back to Devore's a few days later. Paid the big bucks and tip, and then tried on a few jackets and slacks. The economic investment in the haircut netted me a tidy nest egg that tided me over until my next part came along.

• • •

Mickey had invited me to drop by for some ice cream at the Carousel, and being warm, I took off my jacket and hung it over the back of my chair. Ever observant, Mickey immediately noticed the Sy Devore label.

"Nice drapes, that Sy Devore, but din't you get this a few months back at Zeidler & Zeidler?"

"Well, you're right, Uncle Mickey. See, I've got a little scam going with these labels."

My detailing how I'd put together my petite larceny at first drew looks of humorous contempt from Joe, Phil, and Fred, and then—as I described going into Schwab's—howls of laughter.

"'S'great, Kid." Freddy could barely contain himself. "You're using that little pansy Ricky Nelson as your front man. An' he don't even know it!" Again, gales of laughter. Even the normally deadpan Joe Sica chuckled.

Phil was wiping tears from his eyes with his chocolate-stained napkin. "Jeez, ya gotta love it. He's turnin' inta a regular wiseguy."

Mickey leaned forward and tapped my chest. "Nah, nah; you gotta think big. You got a legitimate little grift going here. But, see, ya gotta find a way to get those labels in bunches. Ya gotta take care of one of those tailors, or the janitor, even. See, they're workin' folks. They can always use an extra buck. Ya gotta make it attractive." He looked at me, shaking his head. "Devore labels, whaddaya know."

"Better watch out from your little proto-jay, Mickey." Freddy reached over and dog-rubbed the top of my head. "Next he'll be counterfittin' Good Humor's free ice-cream sticks."

Good Humor ice-cream trucks traversed every neighborhood in Los Angeles with their chime bells playing an annoying little tune that attracted kids like the Pied Piper. To stimulate return business, they randomly inserted a stick marked "free" into batches of their chocolate-coated ice-cream bars, entitling the lucky finder to free ice cream.

My reaction was part embarrassment and part amazement. Embarrassed that they'd had so much fun at my expense over my simple little crime, but amazement that Mickey had so quickly sized up the fundamental economic flaw. Volume.

With my next haircut due, I made an appointment with Sy Devore's barber, and after a not-quite-as-good-as-Al's-but-far-more-expensive haircut and tip, I requested a tour of the tailor's shop. Ushered into the small work-area crowded with sewing machines, big steam pressing irons, and several tailors hard at work, I saw a series of mannequins labeled with names including Sinatra, Martin, Davis, and Lawford.

"You mean they don't even have to come in for a fitting?" I asked.

The eldest of the tailors, wearing a yarmulke with a yellow measuring tape draped around his neck and straight pins stuck in his vest, smiled at my naive question. "No, sir, they just select color and material." He pointed to a wall rack with hundreds of bolts of imported fabrics. "And we have the very best," he added with pride.

On the floor by one tailor's bench another elderly man with white hair was sweeping up a pile of cuttings, discarded buttons, and a couple of labels attached to linings that had been removed. I felt like a gold-rush miner who'd just panned a couple of nuggets and knew he was close to the mother lode.

Thanking the master tailor, I exited, looked up and down Vine, counted buildings, and then headed down to Sunset, turning right, and then another right into the alley behind Wallach's Music City, Hollywood's biggest music store.

Walking up the alley, I counted the buildings until I was outside what I thought must be Devore's. Settling down on a low window ledge and leaning up against the bars, I smoked cigarette after cigarette, occasionally checking my watch.

Finally, just before five, the shop's back door opened and the white-haired old man stepped out, dragging a trash can. Taking a deep breath, I threw my best punch.

"Sir, I was wondering if I could buy some of those labels from you?"

He looked at me as though I had a large hole in my head, and by peering in he was clearly able to determine that there were no brains inside.

"You, too, sonny? I just can't comprehend why these damn labels mean so much. Don't you know that it's the quality of the fabric and the talent of the tailor that make that label worth something?"

"You, too?" Does that mean I'm not the first guy to think this up?

"So, same for you as the other fella. One hundred bucks for a role of one hundred. No more, no less. And cash money. Tonight when I'm done, maybe in an hour, you meet me down the block outside a' Music City."

Our deal cemented, I rushed off to make the bank before closing time.

35

BLOOD ON MY HANDS

"**K**ID, YOU TAKE your car. Fred can go with you, and Joe's going with me."

We pulled away from 705 Barrington up onto Sunset and headed east to Highland. Mickey wanted to see what the Fountain Lanai looked like, and as we drove up, John Ashley was coming out of the underground garage. He recognized my car and waved.

"Mickey's still thinking about getting a place for Candy here," Fred said. "Place okay by you?"

"Sure. It's cool. People are friendly, but nobody's nosy. Lot of showbusiness people. You can enter from the front or the back."

"This guy Ashley. You like him? How much older'n you?"

"Maybe five, six years. And yeah, he's a stand-up guy."

We turned up into the Hollywood Hills behind the Hollywood Bowl.

"Lotsa places wit' For Sale signs round here," Fred observed. "How's come?"

"I hear the real-estate market in this area's pretty slow. Anybody can afford it is moving out of these older parts of Hollywood."

Many of the larger houses showed signs of deferred maintenance, paint peeling on eaves, lawns if not overgrown at least in need of watering and trimming, hedges turning brown.

"Where they goin'?" Fred was looking thoughtful.

"Beverly Hills, Brentwood, Pacific Palisades; that whole area around the Riviera Country Club's big right now."

Ahead of us, Mickey slowed, signaled, and pulled into the driveway of a large two-story house behind two Cadillacs and an older, beautifully-cared-for La Salle limousine. On either side of the front door were two stone griffins. Two guys each the size of Primo Carnera emerged from the La Salle. I hadn't seen them since the first night I'd met Mickey, more than a year ago, but they instantly recognized me and nodded. I did my little tuff-guy nod, and they opened a thick, iron-strapped wooden gate in an ivy-covered wall to one side of the garage.

My little shoulder devil's pointed tail tapped my earlobe. *Pretty mysto, kiddo. Obviously, standing around ringing the front door bell's contraindicated.*

We walked into a rose garden. Standing outside on a narrow terrace with his hands on the door handles of two tall French doors was a familiar-looking figure wearing a tuxedo. I did a quick double take. He was a dead ringer for the Villa Capri's maître d'.

"Nize to zee you, Herr Cohen. You vill find efreybody upstairs in der muzic room."

Music room? Maybe a string quartet? I thought, looking at Bernard. He may have been nicely attired, but there was something else about him, the thickness of his shoulders, the thick wrists extruding from his immaculate French cuffs, the undisguised military bearing.

"Please to komm zis vay." The accent was distinctly more Munich than Vienna with a little touch of what? Waffen SS?

Bernard led us through the house's formal foyer, where a sweeping staircase with a gleaming banister led to the second floor. I followed Joe, who followed Mickey, and we "ascended" the staircase. It was much too elegant to just walk up.

At the end of the long hall, Mickey and Joe stood aside, and I opened a beautifully paneled mahogany door.

Instant Vegas.

Directly in front of us were three blackjack tables with five or six people seated at each. To one side a crap table, with another group clustered around it, and on the other side, a well-attended roulette table. In one corner was an L-shaped bar, and in the other, three black musicians playing a piano, bass, and guitar.

"Whaddaya think?" Mickey said with a little touch of pride in his voice.

"I'm impressed," I said, shaking my head. "It's my first den of iniquity."

Mickey looked at Joe. "See, I told you. Send that niece of yours to a private school like he went to, and she'll have a real good vocab-a-lary."

We followed Mickey through the cigarette and cigar smoke to the bar. Seated with her back to us was an attractive young woman in a dark blue cocktail dress. Mickey touched her shoulder and she turned, smiling up at him. "Oh, hello, Mr. Cohen. How nice to see you again."

I stopped, almost bumping into Joe Sica's back. It was Sherry, the girl I'd taken home from the Chateau Marmont. The one that sadistic son of a bitch Stern had beaten. She smiled warmly at me and lifted her martini glass in a little toasting gesture. *I'm okay, see?*

"May I get you something, sir?" the bartender asked. "Cuba Libre," I said. Somebody had recently clued me in to the fact that this was the official name for a rum and coke.

"How have you been?" I turned back to find an older man wedging in between us. Her eyes met mine for a brief moment. *Sorry, business is business.* He half pulled her off the stool toward the roulette table.

I smiled back. *Another time, maybe.* If she lived to see another time. I watched her back, shook my head, and recalled a few bars of the Chet Baker song "But Not for Me."

There were, however, other attractions. I headed toward the card tables, guided by my little shoulder devil's admonition: *When in a place of action, get some action.*

Fred appeared, and I could see him looking for me. I lifted my hand, and he gave me a little *over here* toss of his head.

"What's up?" I asked. Fred lifted his eyebrows and shrugged. *Business.*

I followed him out and down the hall toward the staircase and another hall that led to another wing of the building. Fred opened another beautiful mahogany door and held it open for me to enter. Joe was inside and pushed the door closed behind us.

Standing before us was Mickey, legs spread, hat off, leather-gloved left fist balled around a roll of quarters, and arm cocked. On the floor was the Fat Man. Blood trickled from what was left of his nose and torn ears; a tooth hung out of the ruined pulp of his mouth on a thread of bloody tissue. One eye was completely shut and his brow gashed open; the other was so bloodshot it looked as if the eyeball had been ruptured.

Mickey kicked him in the groin, and he groaned and rolled away, his back to us, and the obvious stain from his loosened bowels and bladder was spreading through his pants onto the carpet.

"Who the fuck you think you are, you fat fuck. Holdin' out on me. I oughtta kill ya." Mickey's right foot lifted for another kick.

In a swift move, Joe's arms encircled the enraged and out-of-control Mickey. "Mickey! Stop a'fore ya kill this prick."

"This prick needs killin'. I had him at my house, set him up with the cops, with protection, and he fucks me over anyways?" Mickey wrenched loose from Joe and aimed another kick at the Fat Man's spine.

"Jesus! Mickey! Stop fer Chrissakes! He's out. He can't feel nuthin'; Bernard'll take over from here. Let's get out before he croaks."

Joe went behind a large walnut desk to the left of Mickey, pulled open several drawers, and finally found what he was looking for. He held the struggling Mickey while Fred leaned over the Fat Man and tried rolling him over. His four-hundred-pound bulk resisted Fred's first two attempts. Frustrated, Fred looked at me.

"Jesus, this piece of shit-meat's too fuckin' heavy."

Mickey—eyes bulging and the veins in his temples distended—tried to shoulder Joe aside. "Lemme at the bas—"

"He ain't breathin', Mickey! Kid—grab his legs, help me roll him—ready?"

Response to direct order. Bend, grab.

Fred squatted. "One, two, three!" We heaved.

Beneath him, soaked with blood, was one of those small leather satchels I'd seen before.

"Take that and lock it in your trunk. C'mon, Mickey. We gotta get outta here."

"Wait a minute. I *gotta* wash my hands," Mickey announced. I glanced down at the Fat Man. If he was alive, he showed no sign of it. I looked at Fred and Joe. Joe walked over to the desk and retrieved what looked to me like two book-keeper's account ledgers. Fred pulled out a handkerchief and wiped his hands and the doorknob, the door, and the doorjamb, and then went to the desk, wiped over its surface, and, finally, brushed off his suit and straightened his tie.

Mickey finally emerged, and we left the room single file. Bernard appeared at the top of the stairs. Mickey spoke a few words to him. He nodded but didn't click his heels together or give the fascist salute.

It was late, and this time we left by the front door. I noticed the exterior lights weren't on. At my car, I needed to set the bag down so I could fish out my keys and open the trunk. My fingers had bonded to the blood-soaked satchel's handle and wouldn't come unglued. I spit on my fingers, gathered more saliva, spit again, and then again.

Holding the satchel's handle close to my mouth, I started to spit again—got a snoutful of the smell of blood and whatever else had mixed with it, and without warning retched so hard I splattered the Pontiac's back bumper and my shoes.

Tearing the satchel from my hand and pulling some skin from my fingers, I threw the bag into the trunk, spitting again and again now that the saliva was flowing, trying to get the taste of the vomit from my mouth.

Fishing out a Parliament, I steadied myself to light it, started the car, and drove back down the hill to the neon-washed streets of Hollywood.

36

CONFLICTING EMOTIONS

Letting myself into the apartment quietly, I could see Johnny's bedroom door wide open. No writhing bodies. The bed was made. As usual, the amorous Mr. Ashley wasn't home.

It was ten thirty, and I didn't want to be alone. I desperately needed someone to talk to. My first reflex was to call my father. I picked up the telephone and then put it back in its cradle—staring at my hands. My wrists, fingers, and the edges of my sleeves were caked with dried blood. I had to get the gore off me.

Taking a long, hot shower helped, but I couldn't release the pressure. In my car's trunk was a leather bag—with a murdered man's blood all over it. My mind kept replaying the scene of Mickey kicking the Fat Man, of him lying there with his face beaten to a bloody pulp. And I felt guilty.

Something was wrong. I couldn't identify or articulate it. I couldn't release the roiling fear I felt, either. Why was I doing this? I looked in the half-steamed bathroom mirror, and a pleasant-faced kid who looked more like fifteen than twenty peered back at me, not a "Tuff guy," not some small-time hood.

I brushed my teeth for the third time, trying to erase the taste of bile. I could still see the Fat Man's blood under my fingernails. Finding a nail file, I dug at the dark evidence of my complicity, then put toothpaste on a nailbrush and scrubbed them clean.

I'd witnessed a murder. While it was happening I'd shut down emotionally, gone numb. Now it was hitting me like a hard Pacific swell slamming into a seawall, backwashing, and slamming again.

Sitting on the edge of the bathtub, I tried to put Humpty Dumpty back together again. But all the king's horses, and all the king's men's unions were on strike tonight.

The phone rang. *Mickey? No, no, no, I thought. I can't do it. I can't go over there again tonight. I can't hold it together.*

Once. Then after a few seconds once again. Then a third. Jock's code.

I grabbed a towel and sprinted for the nightstand by my bed.

"Hey, Steve, what's—"

"Jock, man, where are you?" I cried.

"I'm over at Fred Tatum's with Lockwood. We're just getting ready to leave. We're going to go to Zucky's in Santa Monica. Get some corned-beef sandwiches and apple pie."

"I'll meet you in twenty minutes."

● ● ●

They were closer, but I beat them. I was climbing out of my car in the tiny parking lot when they pulled up in Lockwood's 1949 Merc woody with his surfboards sticking out the back.

"What's going on, man? You sounded like you'd seen a ghost." Jock put his arm over my shoulder as we walked in.

"You can say that again," I said. "But don't. I might have."

As we sat down, a waitress brought us coffees and took our orders. I wasn't hungry, but the hot coffee helped, and just seeing Jock's concern eased the pressure.

"Let me get this straight, you actually saw a ghost?"

"Worse, I think I saw someone becoming one."

They both looked at me.

"Mickey," I said. "Some kind of gambling setup he's running up in the Hollywood Hills in a big old house. Some guy—I think he runs the place—I mean, it's full of roulette and crap tables, a bar, everything, and he'd been cheating Mickey and Mickey caught him and beat the shit out of him."

"And you're sure he was dead?" Craig asked. "Anybody take a pulse?"

"We touched him. We had to roll him over. I mean, the guy's, like, huge. His face was wasted. He'd pissed and shit himself. He was bleeding from his ears. Fuck, I don't know—"

They sat staring at me, uncomprehending. *I was a traveler, returned from another continent. Telling tales of blue-skinned men.*

"I feel like all I want to do is get the hell outta Dodge."

"What'd happen if you did? I mean, why can't you?" Craig was staring at me now.

"I can't. Mickey gave me the money. I gotta get it back to him."

"Money? You gotta be kidding," Jock said. The waitress arrived with our orders, set them down, and left. Nobody touched the food.

"No. No. These guys are no joke. I'm like their mascot. I do things like run errands, pick up Mickey's dry cleaning. I picked up a guy at the airport and took him to a hotel once. A bad guy. Last night after Mickey killed the fat guy, he gave me something, a bag—money, probably—to hold. They know where I live, what kind of car I drive, probably the license plate, everything. They trust me."

Jock looked at Craig and back to me.

"And you trust them?" Lockwood asked.

Trust? I remembered Mickey last night standing over the

body on the floor. And the night he knocked me on my ass. I heard myself answering yes, but something inside, so deep I couldn't touch it and pull it out, said *no.*

"In a way. But their whole scene's weird. There's degrees of loyalty, but if they were even to suspect—let alone know—I did anything that could cause them a problem—"

Craig shook his head. "Cohen's in a shitload of trouble, Steve. That editor at the *Examiner* says there's like a federal indictment hanging over his head. There's a bunch of political wrangling; apparently he had some cops and a few politicians in his pocket, but that's not going to save him anymore. He's going down. And you will, too."

Jock leaned back in the booth and put his hands over his eyes for a moment. "Steve. We just came from Fred Tatum's. His dad's the CEO at Disney. There're no secrets in Hollywood."

"His younger sisters, Vernette and Melantha, are in classes with some of the Mousketeers at HPS," Craig added. "People are talking about you. It'll get back up the line. Stuff like this always does."

I picked my pack of Parliaments up off the table and shook one out to light.

"Steve, man. Look at yourself." Jock reached over and tapped my wrist. "You've smoked seven cigarettes since you've been here. Your hands shake every time you light one up. You've got to get out of this."

"I can't, Jock. Even if I could, I wouldn't know how."

"Steve," Craig began, his voice edged with concern, "this isn't like rats deserting a sinking ship, either. This is you swimming free before the suction pulls you under."

"He's right, Steve," Jock said. "You've got to go somewhere, get out of here."

But I knew I couldn't, no more than I could just walk away. There was no running. Where would I go? What would I do?

The only world I knew was Hollywood. My career was just getting going again. I couldn't leave.

Something else was anchoring me to Mickey. My ego's stubborn, immature reluctance to examine and admit what that was—an irrational mix of undeserved dependence, ill-deserved admiration, and well-deserved fear—was like a pair of chains binding me to him.

"I can't explain it. But I just can't see a way to do it. It's like chickening out."

Jock shook his head. "Chickening out? What, are you nuts? Since when is getting out of the clutches of a guy who kills people for money chicken? Sticking around's chicken."

"Jock's right, Steve. Cohen's a corrupt degenerate. By keeping that money for him, you've made yourself complicit. He did that for a reason."

"Reason? What do you mean?"

"He bought your silence with your own loyalty. Can't you see that?"

I shook out my last Parliament, crumpled the pack, tossed it into the already full ashtray, and went to the cigarette machine for another pack.

What I wasn't saying, wasn't even capable of getting words around let alone articulating, was that for some completely irrational emotional reason, I was sacrificing myself for some misconceived sense of loyalty to a sociopathic user who kept me around for his own amusement—to pull out, dust off, watch dance, and toss an occasional ego-building tidbit.

Jock and Craig were friends, good friends, but they'd grown up in a different world than I had. They'd never fought for a place in the dugout, let alone the starting lineup. Theirs wasn't a world in which a strong personality, a director, a producer, a casting director, called the shots, and to whom you had to pay attention, do the right things to get noticed and get the part. Though we all shared common moral values, nothing had ever tested theirs, and they simply didn't understand that knowing the difference between right and wrong, good and bad, didn't always mean that making the choice was easy.

And while I suspected all of this, I couldn't phrase it to myself in terms that broke through the emotional wall I had constructed around my relationship with Mickey.

Lockwood got up. "Personally, I don't want to know any more about this. Any of it. Remember last year? All I did was leave my old car outside your place, and Jock and I were both rousted. We didn't know shit then. LAPD does that again, and what are we supposed to do? Rat you out to them? I'm in school, with a city job. I'm engaged. Forget it. I don't want to be in that position. I'd lose everything, including your friendship. But that's nothing compared to what you could lose."

• • •

We paid the bill and walked out into the soft Santa Monica night. Saying good-bye, I pulled out of the parking lot and drove alone up the coast to Malibu. I wasn't ready for bed, and spent the next few hours walking barefoot along the Pacific's edge, watching the moon sink.

Jock was loyal, but Craig was right. I had the most to lose, and in losing that, I would lose everything—freedom, my career, Dad's respect. How would I stand up to being dragged downtown for questioning? Could I hold out? And with an indictment about to come down on Mickey, they'd be looking for witnesses. That would mean cutting a deal to avoid jail time, and then having to spend a lifetime looking over my shoulder.

With the blunt edge of the half-moon gone, Venus followed, into the sea. Behind me, edging over the Santa Monica Mountains, was the first gray smear of dawn.

Finally, still unable to consolidate my conflicting emotions, I headed back to Hollywood and, still dressed, fell exhausted onto my bed and into a troubled sleep.

37

SPECIAL DELIVERY

Sunlight was pouring in my bedroom window.

I reached for the ringing phone and managed to knock it off the nightstand. Leaning over the bed, I grabbed for the handset.

"Hey, Kid, you okay?"

"Uh . . ." I struggled to get the phone to my ear. "Yeah, Uncle Mickey. I'm good."

"Well, that's good. Now, you got that present for me from last night?"

"Sure thing, Uncle Mickey."

"So what I want is you to meet me at the Carousel. Three thirty, four. You okay with that? No auditions? Good, now you're gonna get a call right after this, and you see you take care of that first, okay?"

"Okay. No auditions. I'll be there."

Mickey had a tone in his voice that was a mix between all business and something that sounded suspiciously like concern. I replaced the handset and struggled to sit up in my rumpled clothing. Then the phone rang again.

"Stevens? This is Jack Dahlstrum; I have some good news for you. I've worked out a nice deal with the district attorney for you. I'll need you downtown in the court right after lunch. That work for you?"

"You bet, but what's the deal?" I dreaded his answer, afraid he was going to say something like, *Oh, ninety days in the L.A. County jail, and a small fine, say, twenty-five hundred.*

"Relax. You have no prior record, so I got the DA to reduce your charge to disturbing the peace. You'll show up in court, plead guilty, and pay a twenty-five-dollar fine. Now, that good enough?"

"But—how? How'd you do that?"

"Clever legal beagle that I am, I read the arrest report. The arresting officer said he saw the gun lying on the pavement at your feet. That right?"

"Yes. It slipped through my waistband and fell onto the street."

"In plain view?"

"Right at my feet."

"So the weapon, when observed, was in plain view. Lying right there? Just as the officer reported?"

"Uh-huh."

"Now, he didn't see the firearm concealed, and you weren't carrying it when he observed it. It was in plain view. Not a felony in California."

"Th-thanks."

"You can thank Mickey. He wanted you to avoid the six-month sentence that they could easily have nailed you with. Be thankful for his generosity. Now, you'll need to be in court, in front of the judge to plead, so don't be late."

Late? Leaping out of bed and into the shower, I grabbed a quick egg sandwich at the Sunset Grill and arrived outside the L.A. Superior Court Building on Temple Street in downtown Los Angles and was sitting outside the courtroom before it reopened at one. An hour later the bailiff called my name, and I rose and stood before the judge.

"Mr. Stevens, how do you plead?"

"Guilty as charged, Your Honor."

"The fine will be twenty-five dollars. Please arrange to pay the clerk."

● ● ●

Jumping onto the Hollywood Freeway, I exited on Melrose, took a shortcut down to Wilshire, and arrived at the Carousel at exactly three thirty. Mickey's Caddy was parked in front, and inside, sitting at one of the little round tables, was Itchy.

"You're right on the button, Kid. Folla me." He stood up and led me around the big glass counter with spiral cardboard tubs of ice cream in twenty different flavors. Through a doorway was a utility room, and at the end another door leading to a small office. Mickey Jr. greeted me at the door with an appreciative sniff and my cursory leg hump.

Mickey, on the phone, unlit cigar chomped firmly in place, swiveled around to greet me. "Kid, justa minute. Be right with ya."

Itchy was leaning against a file cabinet, no doubt recalling an Elizabeth Barrett Browning sonnet. I stood, nervously shifting my weight from one foot to another. Hanging up, Mickey turned back to me.

"So you got my little present?"

Sir, yes, sir! Present secure and ready for delivery, sir. Where shall the private deliver it, sir?

"In the trunk of my car, Uncle Mickey."

"You never touched it? Din't open it?"

"Never. Just like you gave it to me."

"An' you don't know what's in it, right?"

"Wasn't told; didn't ask."

"Good, now you go with Itchy back to my place. I'll be by in a few."

Was it some kind of pop quiz? Was there some reason I couldn't go out to my car, take it out of the trunk, and hand it to him here? Didn't ask, didn't dwell. Just wanted to get rid of the goddamn thing.

• • •

A few minutes later I parked around the corner from 705 Barrington, retrieved the little satchel, still tacky with blood—and probably plenty of my fingerprints—and walked over to Itchy, who was standing by his car.

"Here you go." I held it out. Itchy declined it with a shake of his head.

"Now, here's a little word to the wise, Kid. Somebody entrusts you with something, you never give it to anyone except the person it's intended for. Unnerstand?"

Chastened by this obvious reminder of underworld etiquette, I nodded and followed him up the stairs to Mickey's place. Phil Packer opened the door, and inside at the bar was Fred, who gave me a nod and a smile simultaneously. It must have been the extra Annette pictures I'd recently provided.

Then I stopped, and if my jaw didn't hit the floor it was only because I almost stumbled into the coffee table. Off to my left on one of the two enormous couches was the Fat Man.

Well, it wasn't because I *recognized* the familiar contours of his handsome countenance. No, a good many bandages covered the top of his head and eyebrow. His ear was a separate masterpiece of fine surgical dressing. His lips looked like liver stitched together here and there, and it was obvious his jaw was wired.

I avoided making eye contact with his one undamaged eye. Both of his hands were also bandaged. It must have been the lid on the Cohen cookie jar slamming shut.

I made a detour around the offending end of the coffee table, walked up to the bar, sat down, and placed the bag between my feet.

"We heard you did good last night," Phil said, joining me.

"He done okay, just fine," Fred volunteered.

"That makes up for the stupid thing with the gun, yeah?"

I could only hang my head and shake it. Huck Finn, sternly but somewhat warmly berated by Aunt Polly.

Mickey came in, closed the door, walked past Fat Man, and motioned me to follow. Like a spaniel with a duck in its mouth, I went down the hall, wondering if there would be a pat on the head or a fist in my kisser.

I held out the bag, and Mickey pointed to the dresser. "Over there. You know, I watched you last night. You acted good for an actor. You handelt yourself good. Very professional. Must be what you learned sellin' papers, huh?" He pinched both my cheeks and stuffed some bills into my shirt pocket.

"So, you seen Fats out there? Now, don't get no impression I'm going soft. I need him to run that joint. He's a gambler. He knows all the games, all the cons, all the grifts. He's got a fol-lowin'. An' now, he's a lot wiser than he was twenty-four hours ago. 'Course, he won't be dealing cards until they take the casts off, but we din't break but one finger on each hand."

Break a finger? Break the news. EXTRA, EXTRA, READ ALL ABOUT IT! NEWSBOY NOT A MURDER WITNESS.

"So, see, Uncle Mickey ain't so bad a guy, after all. Whyn't you join us tonight at the Formosa."

38

A JURY OF HIS PEERS

NOBODY COULD EVER accuse the Formosa Café, on Santa Monica Boulevard across from Samuel Goldwyn Studios, of being impressive.

Located just west of La Brea Avenue—it was a funky little place, built around an old 1902 Southern Pacific railway car— the Formosa served good but average food and superb drinks. However, Formosa's clientele was impressive, a fact amply documented by the hundreds and hundreds of studio publicity photos lining its walls. Everyone who was anyone or had been anyone or would be anyone had their face in a little black frame on those walls.

Mickey had told me to meet him at nine thirty—early for Mickey, the consummate night owl, so I had a chance to relax and look around a little. George Jessel, the enduring comedian, and the *Herald-Examiner*'s Harrison Carroll—who'd recently given me a line in his popular column—had just taken a seat when Mickey, Phil Packer, and Beverly Hills, a Club Largo stripper with assets in the Candy Barr category, walked in and were seated a booth away.

As I walked over, Carroll gave me a wave. "How are you, Steve? Hey, I hear you're batching with John Ashley; that true?"

Tidbits kept the gossip columnists going, and if you supplied them, they mentioned you. *Up-and-coming young actor Steve Stevens reports that Hollywood's very energetic and available bachelor John Ashley, who recently finished . . .*

Mickey noted our exchange. "Hey, you know that guy, huh? You're coming up in the world."

Lem Quon, the Formosa's owner, showed up with a tray of drinks, and Mickey introduced us. "Steve, when Lem was a kid, before the war, workin' here as a cook, I usta run book outta the back, and I kept all the dough in his safe."

Laughing, Lem turned as Ozzie, Harriet, and Ricky Nelson walked past us to a booth just across the room. "Mickey, I'll see you later. You want the chicken chow mein—as usual?"

"You cook it, Lem; I want it."

Ricky saw me as they were seating themselves and leaned over the back of the booth and waved.

"Who's that?" Mickey asked.

"Mickey, that's Ricky Nelson," Beverly Hills responded. "Haven't you ever watched that *Ozzie and Harriet* show on TV? He's getting really popular as a singer now. Steve, how do you know him?"

"Well," I said, "we hung out together. I was on the show."

I'd spent time at the Nelsons' place just north of Franklin Avenue in Hollywood, as well as at their beach house on Laguna Beach's beautiful Victoria Cove. We'd been close pals.

Ricky started to get up, and I was edging out of the booth when Ozzie turned and looked directly at us. I waved to him, but there was no response. He turned, bent his head toward Harriet, and motioned Ricky to sit down. Sensing something was wrong, I slid back into the booth.

Beverly and Phil both looked at me. As people who had for years been social outcasts, they knew intuitively what they had

Rick Nelson 1956 CADI

STEVE AND RICKY NELSON IN FRONT OF STEVE'S CADDY.

just witnessed. Rejection and stigmatization. If Mickey had noticed the brief nonverbal exchange, he gave no indication.

Somehow, whatever joy the evening might have held for me—and I sensed also for Phil, who of all Mickey's boys was the least gangsterlike—was squelched.

We finished before the Nelsons and passed their booth as we left. I nodded to Ricky. Ricky avoided my gesture. Neither Ozzie nor Harriet even looked up. I took a few more steps and turned, expecting some response from Ricky, if not his parents. They had turned their heads away.

I'd stepped over the line.

Outside, Beverly touched my arm. She was a tall, statuesque brunette, more beautiful in a classier way than Candy.

"Don't take it hard, Stevie. It's like they're in church, and they shut the door to keep you out. I know. People like that have a lotta talent, a lotta success, and a lotta money to show for it, but they have no forgiveness."

Back at the Fountain Lanai, there was a party going on in one of the other places across from the pool. People were standing around with drinks, music was playing, and Sandy, the Sandra Dee body double, spotted me and invited me to join them.

"I've gotta get up for an early interview, but thanks anyhow."

I was in no mood to party. I didn't like the feeling of having been ostracized that I'd carried home with me from the Formosa. It hurt and made me feel tarnished and ashamed.

What would Harrison Carroll be writing in the *Herald-Examiner* next?

"Stevens, with a promising career in film and television, has been increasingly seen in the company of known gangland figures."

And been judged by a jury of his peers.

39
NEW YEAR'S WISHES

"A<small>N' DON' FORGET</small>, we're starting early and running late. Get here before the food runs out."

Rafael Campos's voice on the phone was a welcome surprise. It was going to be one hell of a Hollywood New Year's Eve, and I was in the mood to party. I'd been working steadily for the past few months, with early calls and long days under hot lights. Having a chance to unwind with a friend like Rafael and his wide circle of actors and Hollywood people was more than welcome. Rafael's love of good food and wonderful rum drinks culled from his native Dominican Republic's repertoire promised to be just the combination I'd been looking for.

Putting down the phone, it occurred to me that I hadn't heard much from Mickey recently. Usually he called me at least once a week, but I hadn't had a call for some time. I picked up the phone and dialed.

"Uncle Mickey, it's Steve. Hey, I wanted to know if it'd be okay to drop by."

"Yeah, sure, Kid. Come on over, we'll catch up, okay?"

I showered, changed into a brand-new suit with a new Sy Devore label, and some new loafers—and headed out the door.

Walking up the steps to Mickey's apartment, Abe Phillips, heading down the steps, brushed past me with a sheaf of papers under his arm.

"Happy New Year's, Abe," I said, offering my hand. He neither stopped nor acknowledged me. I'd met him some months back in the LAPD Hollywood Division Station when he'd bailed me out.

Mickey was alone. And he didn't look good. His always neatly pressed clothes were rumpled and stained, his hair looked as though he'd forgotten to comb it, and what was usually only the shadow of his heavy black beard was now a crusty stubble. And Mickey always showered and shaved twice a day.

Abe Phillips hadn't been here on a social call. Putting two and two together added up to a trip "downtown." LAPD had probably pulled him in for questioning. And by the looks of it, the day before.

Mickey pointed to the bar. "Fix yourself something, Kid. Hey, 's'good to see ya. Ya gotta pardon my appearance. Chief Parker's cocksuckers wanned to give me some special season's greetings. Cheer up my new year. They took three shifts to do it."

"I just wanted to stop by and wish you a happy new year. I heard things weren't going so well. I didn't want you to think that was why I hadn't been around. You've always been there for me."

"Going well? Hell. They grab me off the street like a criminal, cuff me, toss me in the back of a cop car somebody just puked in, and then shout shit at me—do I know this, did I do that. Fuck, I told them Billy Graham offered me fifty grand to change my ways, become a Christian, and I like the man, Kid. But I ain't no hypocrite. This bad Jew woun't make a good Christian, 'cause he ain't no good as a Jew."

He threw up his arms, mumbled something, sat down, and got up.

"I can't sit in my house like this, fer chrissakes. Lookit what they done to me! Treat me like a bum an' give bums like Parker and that ass-kissin' Mayor Bowron a pass. And all the favors, all the money, all the little deals I done for them."

He stopped, looked at me. "You want a drink, Kid? Go. Make one. You know they got the FBI, the FBI coming to talk to me, that little fag cocksucker J. Edgar Hooooo-ver. Lookin' to settle some goddamn score with Kefauver."

I'd never seen Mickey like this, and the combined shock of his appearance and disjointed rambling reminded me uncomfortably of my mother's early stages of mental illness. What could I say or do for a person who was falling apart? I wanted to go and put an arm over his shoulder, talk to him, try to calm him down, but I was afraid. Mickey wasn't the kind of man you put an arm around. And at some level, I feared that in this state he could turn on me.

He paced back and forth from the bar to the big window, looked out into the deepening dusk, and turned and paced back.

"See, Kid, the only fuckin' thing the government can get me on is fuckin' taxes. That's it. Ha-ha-ha. The shits. If they only knew, the dumb bastards. And where's my friends back East? How come that phone's not ringing?"

I half sat on the barstool, trying to figure out how to get out and feeling simultaneously guilty that I wanted to abandon him. But the truth was I could neither help Mickey nor endure being around him, witnessing his obvious distress and psychological disintegration.

It was as if his power was draining out of him—as if he was deflating.

He mumbled something about cleaning up and turned to leave the room. I stood up and thrust my hand out.

"Uncle Mickey, you take care of yourself, okay?" I let myself out and walked slowly down the steps to my car.

As I was starting to get in, two men appeared. Suits, hats, brown thick-soled shoes. One put his hand on the Pontiac's door handle, covering it, and took my car keys.

"Hold it," the other growled. "Let's see some ID." He held up his left hand. His black badge case held the now-familiar LAPD shield.

He took my wallet, glanced at my California driver's license, and put it in his jacket's outside pocket.

"Step over here. We want to talk to you." His partner grabbed my right wrist and cuffed it to my left without putting my hands behind me.

He pushed me into the back of an unmarked 1956 Ford and climbed in beside me. He made Jack Webb or Broderick Crawford—the big cop TV heroes of the time—look like Mr. Rogers.

The other detective climbed in behind the wheel.

"So you're Stevens? Big tough-guy movie star? That you?" Before I could answer, he put a hard right into my ribs so suddenly it knocked the wind out of me. I bent forward reflexively.

"Nah. Not so tough, are we? You little shit punk." The next blow was expertly delivered to the area just above my belt line and under the floating rib on my left hip.

His partner chuckled and started the car, driving slowly up Barrington.

"See, we've been looking at you for a while, and you know, frankly, son, we just don't really like what we're seeing. Now, I don't know or care what your deal is with that pudgy little fuck; maybe you're sucking his dick, maybe he's sucking yours, but we're going to find out just how fucking tough a tough guy you really are."

His next blow hurt worse than the other two. He expertly slapped my left cheek in such a way that my nose made an audible crack as if it had exploded, and I felt the pain go through my body like a hot poker. The next punch closed one eye.

My head was spinning, and I started choking and spitting up the blood. Some of it must have splattered on his arm, and he stiff-fingered my ribs again. My hands went up, and the edge of one of the cuffs caught his hand and nicked his eyebrow.

"You little fuck!" He'd hit me twice before the driver reached over and grabbed him. "Knock it off, Sam! He's bleeding too much," he yelled and pulled over.

He exited and came around to open the back door and pull me out, then removed the cuffs and shoved me across the sidewalk beneath a tree on somebody's lawn near San Vincente. The big guy tossed my wallet and keys in the gutter.

"Tell the Mick 'Happy New Year from LAPD,' sucker."

Dazed and disoriented, I got to my feet. My suit was a mess, one knee grass-stained, the other torn from contact with the pavement. I summoned up my best images of a brutally beaten man—maybe Bogie—stumbling gamely away from his attackers. But it didn't ease the pain. And there was no applause.

I was only a few blocks from my car—and Mickey's place, but I didn't think of going back in there. Reaching my car, I climbed into the front seat and passed out. It was nearly dawn when I woke up and managed to start the car and get back to the Fountain Lanai.

I was afraid to go to the local hospital's emergency room, thinking they might have to report me to the cops. What would I tell them? The cops did it? Unlikely.

I still had the number of Sherry, the girl that sadist Stern had beaten, and needing someone who knew something about this sort of thing I called, hoping she'd be home on New Year's Day. She was, and she told me to get my face in cold water until she could get there.

She arrived with a little overnight case full of potions, lotions, and pain pills, and spent an hour doctoring me. She poured some white powder into a glass and made me drink it, put me to bed, and disappeared.

I woke up—twenty-four hours later.

40

REAPPEARANCE

Looking in the mirror for the tenth time in two hours, I saw that nothing had changed.

It was now three days into January, and the puffy eyes were much better. The semicircular black bruises under them could be covered by pancake makeup. No problem there. The problem was my still-swollen and tender nose. I had to keep the dressing over it.

Somehow, Sherry had put it back in place. The septum still felt wobbly and—when I touched it—still moved. But she'd cautioned me to keep the adhesive tape she'd expertly placed over it in place for a week. I'd done that, but being a house-bound shut-in was getting old.

Normal people faced with such a dilemma would go out, and cheerfully explain to anyone who bothered to notice and inquire that they'd been involved in an altercation.

But this was Hollywood, and I was an actor. Wear makeup out, and everyone would really start looking at my face. And while two black eyes alone could be explained or lied about, an obviously professionally structured application of adhesive tape over the bridge of my nose meant that the truth—that LAPD's finest, while protecting and serving, had somehow managed to create the basis for a choice lawsuit by the ACLU—would be laughed at and dismissed as a fatuous fabrication.

What they'd believe was that I'd visited Dr. Fuch's renowned Beverly Hills proboscis parlor for a nose job. And my vanity wouldn't allow that. A beating by the cops? Sure. But a nose job? No way.

A few hours later, Joe Sica called.

"Th' missus wanned to invite you over to dinner. You available tomorrow night?"

Now here was someone who would absolutely believe my story.

"Sure, Joe. Love to get out of the house. What time and where?"

• • •

Joe and his wife lived in a newer apartment building in the 1700 block on Las Palmas. The place was nicely if not richly decorated. Mrs. Sica's Italian heritage showed in her preferences in ceramics and antiques. I'd arrived with flowers, and Mrs. Sica looked pleased and introduced me to a girl who'd been standing in the background.

"Steve, this is our niece's friend, Alice. She's just turned sixteen and wants to get started as an actress. Perhaps you can give her some tips? Now, I hope you've brought a big appetite with you."

"You bet, Mrs. Sica," I said. I could see Joe looking at my face, but he said nothing.

At dinner I noticed the conversation distinctly avoided any mention of Mickey, and instead, probably because of the girl, centered on what I'd been doing. Joe actually admitted he'd watched *The Target: Corruptors,* but Mrs. Sica soon steered the conversation back to Annette, whom both she and Alice couldn't hear enough about.

"Could you get me one of her pictures?" Alice asked. I told her I had one in my car, and excused myself to get it for her.

Outside, I saw one of those familiar-looking older, unmarked Fords and two guys in suits. Sica was under surveillance. And, of course, so was I.

My physical reaction was immediate. *When in danger or in doubt, run in circles, scream, and shout.* Back inside, I could feel my heart pounding and my stomach tightening. My bladder suddenly felt as though it was going to burst.

As Mrs. Sica and Alice purred over the publicity photo of Annette holding hands with me, the phone rang. Joe excused himself and went down the hall. I excused myself, heading in the same direction to the bathroom. Just across from it was another room whose door was ajar. Joe's back was to me, but I could clearly hear his words:

"Nah, don' worry. This is not a problem. He's a good kid; you let me take care of it."

I carefully closed the bathroom door, unzipped, and closed my eyes as everything released.

That was me he was talking about. And somebody thought I was a problem.

Getting back to the dining room was like swimming in Jell-O. Mrs. Sica had served a beautiful dessert, but I couldn't begin to face sitting down again. Every fiber in my body screamed, *Get out!* And Joe sensed it.

"Mrs. Sica, the dinner was wonderful. I hope you'll excuse me, but I have a very early interview tomorrow."

Joe walked with me to the apartment's door and stepped through into the outside hall.

"What happened to you?"

"The cops had Mickey's staked out New Year's Eve. I went over to—"

"I can guess the rest from your mug. You say anything? I'll unnerstand, but I gotta know—just in case. We got lawyers."

"No. They didn't even ask me anything; one guy drove around the block and the other played speed bag on my face."

"That's how they start the process. Pick you up, beat you up, and soften you up. You see them again, just like you just did, outside a' here—them guys—and your guts go soft. And they do that a coupla times, until you give 'em what they want. Believe me, I know."

I looked out at the street—the Ford was still there.

"So the word's out. You're on somebody's list. And the grand jury might call you as a witness. So to avoid being subpoenaed, hows about youse take a little vacation?"

"Vacation? Joe, what're you talking about? Would that be legal?"

"Of course. Unless they subpoena you, you can go anywhere you want. An' if they can't find you, they can't call you, right? So, you like Vegas?"

"Vegas? Yeah, sure I like Vegas. A lot."

"So, good. Go home, pack a little suitcase, keep cool, and stay put. You're gonna do a lambster. You changed th' address on your license since you moved last year?"

"Jeez, no. I completely forgot."

"Good. Maybe they know where you're livin', but they don't know you're livin' wit' Ashley yet. But they will if you go out and they follow you back inside, see. So stay put till you hear from me and it's all okay. You got it?" Shaking my hand, he smiled and punched my shoulder. "Take care, Kid."

Walking out, I noticed the Ford was gone.

But not the knot in my gut.

And not the terror.

41

LAMBSTER

Wʜᴇɴ I ɢᴏᴛ home, John Ashley, as usual, was MIA.

I very carefully packed an overnight bag with more than an overnight's wardrobe.

And stayed put.

Around ten thirty there was a knock on my door. Standing outside was a thickset figure in a peacoat and knit watch cap.

"Here's somethin' for ya. I'm waiting outside, so make it snappy. I gotta get youse to Burbank by eleven."

He handed me a thick envelope and did a little bob 'n' shuffle. One of the old fighters Mickey and the boys kept around for errands.

Opening the envelope I found two airline tickets, one a round-trip, to Las Vegas, the other was an undated open flight— and seven one-hundred-dollar bills. Grabbing my bag, I turned off the lights and, like a good little soldier, aimed myself toward the clean-looking little 1957 Chevy two-door waiting at the curb.

Scrapper hummed and I sat silent. He made the trip in

twenty-five minutes, driving fast but carefully. I kept wondering just what was really going on. They were getting me out of town, and I'd picked Las Vegas, but everybody knew the town's reputation. Didn't that make me look guiltier than if I'd gone to Las Vegas, New Mexico?

The Burbank airport still looked like it did in *Casablanca*, and the little DC-3 was nearly empty. I settled back in my seat, put my feet out in front of me, and studied the shoelaces on my Clarke's desert boots. What had Lockwood said about Mickey's pals and associates disappearing whenever grand juries began looking at his activities?

They were fishing. Just fishing. And I was either the fish or the bait.

But even if they hauled me in, lit me up, and smoked my ass like an Alaska salmon, what could I really tell them?

Let's see. Mickey loved the nightlife, tipped everybody well, and got commensurate service for doing it? Owned an ice-cream shop? That he hit me and knocked me down for stupidly carrying a pistol around? That he beat up the Fat Man over something about gambling money? Money I never actually saw. What was that? Witness to an assault? But I didn't see anything but a couple of kicks. I'd seen my share of Perry Mason; some smart lawyer would make mincemeat out of me. And secretly I'd be glad, because while I'd come to dislike Mickey's life and what he did, I couldn't help liking him.

So the worst thing some hotshot DA could do was put me in jail for a few months for disturbing his case. Mickey, however, might take a notion to restrict my motion. That wasn't a comforting thought, even if I tried to make light of it in my darkest hour.

Landing at Las Vegas's little single-runway McCarran Airport was bumpy, and outside in the chill desert air I could see my breath. I'd brought one warm jacket, and I turned the collar up against the cold as I walked off the plane. Not knowing exactly what to expect, I'd carried my little bag, so I didn't have to pick anything up. But that had been taken care of.

"You Steve?" Standing to one side as I walked through the chain-link gate was a guy who must have been close to seven feet tall. What do you say to a man you have to look that far up to? I resisted "How's the air up there?" and nodded.

"I'm Axel. This everything you brung? No other stuff?" He had a smile the approximate width of Hoover Dam, and teeth just slightly smaller than the individual packages of the carton of Parliaments I'd brought for emergencies—like extreme nervousness while being put through a meat processor at the local slaughterhouse.

I hesitated shaking hands. If this guy was my executioner, I didn't want to get too friendly. Besides, walking beside him, I felt like a child of three toddling after a basketball player. Outside the arrival area was a big black Lincoln sedan—the kind with suicide doors. Axel opened the back door with the touch of a button on a solenoid. I tossed my bag across the seat and climbed in. Then he got in beside me. "Guy drivin's Seymour, but his pals call him Frenchie, an' I call him Knucklehead. Ha-ha.'

The lights were on up there in Axel's dome, but the bulb was only 60 watts.

Seymour F. Knucklehead's neck was so short that he had to twist his entire trunk and shoulders around to greet me. "Don't pay attention to this Swedish meatball; there's very little oxygen at his altitude."

"I was wondering about that," I said, trying to be simultaneously cool and humorous, as befitted a man about to go to his—destination? That lasted about fifteen seconds. I'd flown into Las Vegas enough times to know that when you left McCarran Airport, you made a right turn toward town and the Strip. We turned left, toward the desert.

Not a good direction in terms of potential longevity. People, or the remains thereof, were often reported as being found out there. Local papers jokingly called it the "Gangster Graveyard." Some joke. Not even Sy Devore would have called me a gangster.

My mouth went dry. I tried to light a Parliament, but I couldn't pull in enough breath to inhale. It came in short puffs, matched by the long bursts of heart palpitations and guilty recollections of past advice about questionable associations gone unheeded.

Next to me, Axel's impressive bulk loomed like Mount McKinley. Scrunching up against the other door still didn't leave any available room. My left hand searched for a door handle, but there was only a series of buttons. Was there an ejection seat in Lincoln Continentals?

And worse yet, while Frenchie "Knucklehead" Seymour was totally silent, Axel the Impressive was subaudibly whistling through his teeth.

Whistle while you work. You're a fuckin' jerk. Seymour's a weenie, with a little peenie. Bet it doesn't work.

Clever rhymester that I was, prayer was probably futile, but anything was better than nothing, so I began pleading my case to God.

Look, God, I've totally screwed up. Please forgive me for anything I ever did to offend you. Please take into account the good things I did. Mrs. Miller's kitten in the tree? That lost puppy my folks wouldn't let me keep? I never shortchanged anybody when I was selling papers. I know I had sex outside of marriage, but those girls were all willing.

Response from above wasn't immediately forthcoming.

The road had begun to climb into a series of low foothills, barren under the wan light of a crescent moon. The whole landscape looked unreal, like a bad scene from a Roger Corman horror film. If I was going to die, why did it have to be in a place that looked like a bad movie?

I went back to prayer.

"Hey, Seymour." Axel suddenly switched back on. "There's a spot up ahead; pull over there. I gotta piss."

This was it! My bladder was straining, and my anal sphincter was puckered tighter than a pit bull's jaws.

Seymourhead F. Knucklie was doing about seventy, and when the big Lincoln began to pull off the hard surface of the road onto the sand and gravel of the shoulder, Axel's weight was tossed against me as the car fishtailed a little before stopping.

I tried resolute determination to meet my impending fate with grace and dignity. That didn't work. My teeth were chattering too hard to grit my jaw. That left tears and potential pity.

"Uh, any chance we c-can t-talk about this?" I squeaked.

"What. About me taking a piss? You in that big a hurry to get to Vicky's?"

Vicky's? "Vicky's?"

The dome-light went on as Axel opened the left side door, and he noticed the tears streaming down my face.

"Aw, jeez, what's the matter. You don't wanna go to Vicky's?" He looked at Seymour. "Did you get this wrong? Was it Victor's we was supposed—"

Seymour looked crestfallen. "Steve, you okay? What's with the tears? Axel, Jesus, did we make a mistake? Kid, they didn't tell us you was a fag. Aw, I'm sorry. We thought—"

I shook my head. I wasn't getting any of this, and my heart was pounding so hard I couldn't get my thoughts together to respond.

"Axel, you schmuck, the kid here's thinkin' we're takin' him to the farm."

"What? I gotta piss." Axel looked more confused than I was.

"Steve, he's got a weak bladder. Got hit by a cop car last year. So alla time, he's gotta piss."

"You ain't offended, I hope?" Axel looked apologetic.

"No, my bladder's telling me the same thing," I said, sliding out of the Lincoln into the cold desert air. Axel was standing by the car's right-rear fender, both hands lowered to half-mast and his head tilted back in classic male-relief position. I went around the front and assumed the posture.

It was an epic evacuation. I voided with abandon. It was better than the best sex I'd ever had. Followed by a great fart of relief.

And the solid, terrifying sound of a pistol shot.

Dick in hand, my knees gave way. The thoughts rushed through my head at the speed of light. *The bastard! Caught me in this position. So much for dignity. Shoot me like this! What an asshole!*

"Fuckin' snakes!" Axel was screaming. "I fuckin' hate fuckin' snakes!"

I heard a car door slam and Seymour shouting. "Axel, you fuckin' idiot. Put that piece away!"

Seymour was out of the car now, trying to help me to my feet. Somehow I'd managed to zip my fly and regain a modicum of dignity.

"Mary, Mother of God, I thought he shot you." Seymour was trying to brush the gravel off my trouser legs.

"Thanks," I managed to say. I had now, at the age of twenty, achieved the apex of a lifetime's embarrassments. And I didn't need any more.

Think Bogie, my little shoulder angel whispered.

"Got any more snakes you need to shoot, or can we just go before Axel shoots his dick?"

"Yeah, yeah, sorry 'bout that, Steve. Axel—get back in, fer Chrissakes. Kid, you sit up here with me. He don't mean nothin'. He's sorry; I'm sorry. You don't gotta tell Mr. Cohen or nothin', huh? Say, is it true you know Annette?"

How long had it been since Annette? How many miles?

I fished out a Parliament and settled back for the rest of the drive.

42

VICTORIA'S SECRET

SEYMOUR PULLED OFF onto a dirt road with a metal ranch gate and a cattle grate.

Axel got out and opened it, waited while we passed through, and then closed it. Ahead, I could see the lights of a small ranch-style house with the mandatory hitching post and half-buried wagon wheel. We pulled up in front of a row of whitewashed river rocks, and a cactus-lined porch that led up onto the wide porch. The door opened, and the silhouette of a woman appeared against the soft golden glow of a light inside.

"This here's Vicky's place," Seymour said. Axel was still maintaining radio silence after his snake-shooting spree.

I stepped out, reached in and grabbed my bag. Seymour waved sheepishly, and I acknowledged with a nod. He hit the electric window button, backed the big Lincoln up, and drove back down the road. Even in the Mob everyone had to have a job.

Approaching the porch, the woman stepped down to greet me.

"In case Abbot and Costello forgot to tell you, I'm Vicky, and welcome to Rancho Perdue, Steve. I've been expecting you, but knowing those two, I'd resigned myself to a long wait and a longer list of excuses. Please come in. How was your flight?"

"Longer and bumpier than usual."

Stepping inside, I was suddenly aware of the scale of the house and room. It had been hard to tell in the dark, but now, the ranch house's size was apparent. Bigger than I'd thought. And nice. Heavy, hand-hewn rafters, wide polished plank floors. It had everything but Gene Autry and Champion. Monterey-style furniture, Navajo rugs, original paintings, copper lamps with mica shades. Everything looked settled in, comfortable.

"Sweetie, I'm guessing you'd probably like a drink; what's your pleasure?" She gestured to a bar that separated the living room from another room beyond.

"Cuba Libre would be great. And a couple of aspirin. Those clowns are enough to give anyone a headache. God."

"We can certainly do that," she said, stepping behind the bar. "Would you like to freshen up?" She pointed to a door. "In there. Aspirin's in the medicine cabinet."

Coming out, I saw she'd put my drink on the bar on a little coaster and was reaching for a cigarette. I pulled out my old Zippo and snapped off a light. She smiled at me over the flame, inhaled, and exhaled.

"Thank you," she said, and indicated my drink. "I'll join you in a minute; I'm chilling some champagne. You're both much younger and more attractive than I'd been led to believe."

"Are you a friend of Mickey's?"

"Sweetie, in this town"—she made a gesture over her shoulder toward Las Vegas—"if you aren't a friend of Mickey's, you don't have many friends."

She was studying me, leaning back against the back of the bar. I smiled and returned the compliment. She had dark auburn hair and was probably at least forty, but the smooth swell of her Levi's over her hips and thighs and the way her cowboy shirt contoured over her shoulders and breasts suggested a trim, athletic figure.

Like her house, she exuded a quality of comfortable style and a certain relaxed but controlled grace. She'd probably seen more than most, and survived it all. And it was a quality that I found attractive, admirable, and yes—exciting.

"Now," she said, smiling, "there are some ground rules while you're here. Let's go over those so we're both clear."

Not knowing how to respond, I smiled. Probably my best, most sincere boyish smile—with a little chin lift.

She removed a split of Piper from an ice bucket she'd placed on the bar, skillfully twisted the wire, and eased out the cork with the faintest of pops.

"You're *here* because it's better at this time than being *there,* wherever there is. And *why* you're here, and where *there* is, I'd be much more comfortable not knowing if it involves anything illegal, or anything you've done that you probably shouldn't have. *N'est-ce pas?*"

I grinned.

"That cute little grin will take you a long way, but I'm sure you're well aware of that by this stage of your life. Now, I have a woman who lives nearby, June, who comes in and cooks because I don't. Coffee. That's it. But she has children and has to schedule things, so if you want to have a meal, you'll have to tell me or her when, and what you'd like to have. Okay?"

Omitting the cute grin, I nodded sincerely.

"There is a hamper in your closet. You can put your washable clothing in there, and judging from that little bag you brought, there won't be much. Another woman comes in and takes care of that and cleaning. If you don't make your bed, she will. The dry cleaner drives out once a week and picks up any-thing I have that needs cleaning, and delivers it a few days later. Okay so far?"

"Okay so far."

"I have a wonderful pool; do you swim?"

"I swim."

"Did you bring trunks?"

"I didn't."

"Not that *that* matters," she said and winked. "Now, you understand that you are a guest here, not a prisoner.

"You won't have to worry about expenses. Everything's been taken care of. Did anybody provide you any walking-around money?"

"Yes."

"Now, I expect that you'll want to go play some game that includes cards on the Strip, and take in a show or two?"

"Love that."

"Good, we'll plan on that tomorrow night. Even for Las Vegas and especially for me, it's just too late tonight—well, actually this morning."

I glanced at my watch. It was after four.

"When I see a man glance at his watch I make one of two assumptions."

I lifted my eyebrows.

"Either he's tired and wants to get some sleep, or I'm talking too much about things to which he's not willing to listen."

She lifted her beautifully arched eyebrows and tilted her head.

"Um-hum? Thought so. Well, your room's just up those stairs to the right, the covers are turned down, and the night-light's on in case you're afraid of the boogeyman."

Throwing caution to the wind along with shyness—she was probably old enough to be my mother, but embodied all the understated sexuality and sophistication of a Lauren Bacall—I held up my hand.

"Do I get a tuck-in?"

"Not tonight, darling, remember? You have a headache."

• • •

A tapping on my door broke the spell. I'd been lying half-awake on my back, feeling secure and comfortable for the first time in what seemed like years. I could look out the window at a series of low hills, with fences, and here and there something with four legs. Vicky stuck her head in the door.

"Have you slept enough? If you want anything to eat before dinner, now's your chance, June's here."

I threw on the single pair of Levi's I'd brought and a sweatshirt, and went down to find the kitchen. It was almost noon.

• • •

June turned out to be a large blonde woman with the ability to cook huge, delicious breakfasts. Eggs she'd collected from her own henhouse, potatoes cooked with onion, green and red peppers, a small New York steak cooked in a pan with butter, fresh biscuits, and coffee—with cream from somebody's nearby dairy cow.

Vicky seemed to have disappeared, until I found the door that led to a patio outside and the pool. Then all that seemed to have disappeared was Vicky's swimsuit. She was lying face-down on a chaise, acquiring an unobstructed tan.

Torn between stripping as I ran out shouting and diving in and playing it cool, I played it cool. This, after all, was a woman who was obviously no stranger to anything I had to offer or in any rush to even find out if I *had* anything to offer. Nor could I hang out behind the screen door, perving her like a Peeping Tom. Not that I didn't want to, but it was too creepy.

Needing a shower and a shave, I returned to my room, showered, stretched out, and fell fast asleep.

• • •

"We seem to be sleeping well." Vicky was leaning against the dresser. It was early evening, and I'd slept most of the day.

"We have reservations, and we'll need to leave in about an hour, so up and at 'em."

Someone had taken my clothes and hung them in the closet. My slacks and jacket had been freshly pressed. I took another shower, dressed, and was waiting in the living room when Vicky appeared. Elegant. Svelte in a sheath cocktail dress that did nothing to hide the curves I'd seen earlier.

"Wow," I exclaimed.

"Not too bad for an old broad, huh?"

"No, ma'am. Not too bad at all." I nodded appreciatively.

"I'm a graduate of the Mae West school: 'When I'm bad, I'm better.'"

"I'm good with that. There's no such thing as bad enough." It was all I could come up with under the circumstances.

Her late-model Ford Thunderbird was parked outside, and she did the driving. Good company makes any trip shorter, and it seemed as if we'd been on the road only a few minutes before we were pulling up in front of the Flamingo, our supper stop.

And it was obvious from the treatment we received that Vicky was someone special. But depending on who was doing the greeting, or whom we ran into, the name changed. Here she was Mrs. This; Miss Victoria over there; and Mrs. That somewhere else.

She was a model of graciousness. "Thank you, George," or "Why, you're so very kind to think of me, Fred!" or "Without you, Sam, this dive would sink." And always, everywhere, it was "Please follow me; we've reserved the best spot in the house."

One very courtly and distinguished man, probably in his late seventies, with a blackthorn cane and a silk ascot, approached as if she were royalty, took her hand, and gazed reverently into her eyes.

"You know, Victoria, there is never a day goes by I don't think of you and Ophelia, and your wonderful mother and father. She was a saint, and he, my dear, a godsend for our family."

Whoever Vicky was, or had been, she bore more marks of breeding than wear.

I'd been to Las Vegas before with two of my A-list teen friends, Tommy Kirk, Disney's biggest star at that time, and Harry Cohen Jr., whose father was one of the last movie moguls, and we'd been treated well. But this was on another level.

And as the evening progressed, from dinner to the tables, to a show, to another show, to winding up in an intimate lounge featuring the Treniers, a black trio, to approaching alcohol-level horizontal in the front seat of her car, Miss Vicky never faltered.

My next recollection was of waking. Not in my room or my bed, and not alone. And the idyll continued without another human being's intrusion. Swimming followed by sex, uninterrupted for a good many hours on end by nothing but fatigue. None of Miss Vicky's various and imaginative appetites were left unassuaged.

Until the phone rang late on the sixth day.

"Steven, it's for you," she said. "I think this is personal."

She smiled, handed me the phone, and left the room.

"Steve? Hey, it's Phil. You havin' a grand old time with Vicky? No kiddin'? Well, she's a doll and you, my boy, are clean. You aren't on anybody's witness lists. LAPD, State, Feds, nobody! So you can come on home now. Mr. Michael says you did good, okay?"

I hung up, stared at the Charles Wilbourne painting in the

den of a man with a turban on a polo horse. Did I want to leave?

Miss Vicky came in moments later, pinched my cheek, and gave me a *thanks-it-was-grand-but-it's-aloha-time* smooch and said, "I've just made reservations, cutie. I'll drive you to the airport."

Over.

Like that.

43

HOMECOMING

No Scrapper in his Chevy.

No Lincoln limo with Laurel and Hardy gunsels.

Burbank Airport was nearly deserted, but I finally found a cab. My level of importance had obviously taken a tumble. I was on my own.

Back at the Fountain Lanai, there was a note from Johnny. He'd be gone all weekend. I clicked on the radio and turned the dial to KFWB, Station 98. They were playing a recap of Ricky Nelson's biggest hits, including his newest, "Hello, Mary Lou, Goodbye Heart." I hadn't seen him since that night at the Formosa, though I'd called several times. It would be good to see him again, explain.

Picking up the phone, I dialed his number. His answering service picked up the call. I left my number.

"Lonesome Town" was the next cut. I sat there, feeling melancholy, remembering when he'd recorded it, back in 1959.

He was recording a lot now. Probably busy. I'd try calling again, tomorrow.

That lonesome night stretched into days.

I wanted to call Mickey, but with his trial pending, it seemed best that I let him call me. As it turned out, he didn't.

In the next weeks, the daily papers were full of Mickey's progress through his big federal income tax trial. Sometimes I read them; sometimes I couldn't. Sometimes I didn't even want to try.

Many of his boys, including the Sicas, were facing their own trials.

With Mickey on the defensive, with his power base stripped

ANNETTE, STEVE, AND SHELLEY FABARES.

from him and the various state and federal commissions smelling blood, who he was, and what he'd really been and done were subjects of lengthy editorials, television shows, and now national attention.

Jack Dahlstrum, Mickey's attorney, called, cautioning me to avoid any contact with Mickey or anyone whom I knew had been associated with him.

"Steve," he'd warned, "because of everything, you might have your own problems to deal with." It was a prophetic statement.

Weeks stretched into months.

My agent, Hy Sieger, was having difficulty landing me good parts. Ricky Nelson never returned a single call. I never saw him again, and I never appeared again on *The Adventures of Ozzie and Harriet.*

Annette, busy now as America's new sweetheart, was reportedly very busy working, according to her secretary, and didn't have time to talk. Shelley Fabares, whom I had dated briefly—just as friends—became Donna Reed's daughter on *The Donna Reed Show*.

Marlene Willis and I didn't date again. She wasn't interested in resuming our friendship.

Jock Putnam and Craig Lockwood had become a little distant, probably because of my attitude and response toward their concern over my safety. Their own lives and careers were taking them in different directions, and many of our old Hollywood Professional School gang, though in contact, were not as close as we'd once been.

While John Ashley's career continued its steady rise, I soon had to move and didn't see that much of him. *High School Caesar* did well as a drive-in movie, but didn't provide much of a boost for my career.

My family—Dad, Mom, and my brother, Reggie—had relocated to New York for financial reasons.

Eventually Mickey was convicted, sentenced, and packed off to Alcatraz Prison, the infamous "Rock" in San Francisco Bay, to serve a ten-year sentence.

Weathering that long period of rejection and the resulting anxiety and depression had a curious effect. I made the conscious decision to change my life's direction, come to grips with what I'd done, and carry on. With new photos—I was finally looking like I was out of high school—renewed effort, and a series of small parts, a few more important acting jobs came in.

Months stretched into a year.

It helped. Two B-B movies, *Agent from Harm* and *Cobwebs*, helped financially. But *Cobwebs* was never released. And with all of this came a slow realization. Minor acting parts don't make for much of a career. I didn't want to end up hanging out at Schwab's, swapping lies and excuses about my agent's failure, instead of coming to grips with the limits of my own talent.

In 1963 I had an opportunity to redirect my efforts from on the screen to behind the scenes, working myself up from several smaller talent agencies to the Mishkin Agency.

Meyer Mishkin was a Hollywood legend, representing Lee Marvin, Richard Dreyfus, James Coburn, and Jack Palance, among others. Deft with people, and meticulous in looking out for his actors' careers, Mishkin was a profound influence as a mentor. My office overlooked the Sunset Strip, I drove a new Mustang, and my suits no longer bore the purloined Sy Devore labels.

And more years passed.

Marriage followed, children, and a career change to a casting director at Screen Gems, then the opportunity to work with George C. Scott and Stanley Kramer.

Jock had married and had two children, and his career as a successful Hollywood soundman was flourishing. Craig had also married and had a daughter, divorced, and was working nearby as a magazine editor at Peterson Publishing on the corner of Sunset and Doheney.

Sunset Strip was losing its glamour. Hippies—"Strip People," they called them—had trashed the old Strip's gloss and glitter. The big elegant nightclubs closed. Nobody wanted to be seen on a street with druggies and panhandlers. Like an old Hollywood actress whose looks have faded, Sunset was in decline.

Somehow, a decade passed. It was 1974.

And one day the phone rang.

My secretary leaned into my office. "Mr. Stevens, there's a Mr. Michael on line four for you." The hair went up on the back of my neck.

It had been almost fourteen years since I'd spoken to Mickey. There'd been a vicious assault in prison, his health had deteriorated. He'd been released.

"Hi, Uncle Mickey."

"Hey, Kid, what do you know about this Patty Hearst thing?"

A shadowy black radical group, the Symbionese Liberation Front, had kidnapped Patty Hearst, daughter of William Randolph Hearst Jr., from her Berkeley apartment. The newspapers were full of the family's attempts to secure her release. Nothing had worked. Hearst, who had known Mickey, was reaching out to anyone he could possibly think of who might be able to help. His net had dragged in the old and now nearly forgotten mobster.

"You have all them show business connections an' ya might hear some stuff. Find out what you can and get back to me. Remember, Kid, you owe me."

Uncle Mickey's grave.

And he hung up. Like that. Without leaving a number.

How was I supposed to reach him in the unlikely event that I could find anything out? And unlikely was as likely as it was going to be.

I sat stunned, emotions and adrenaline jogging through my mind and body. But in the days after, the weeks, and the months after, he never called again.

• • •

Two years later, on July 29, I picked up the *Los Angeles Times.* An article and old file picture of Mickey in his characteristic hat caught my attention. Uncle Mickey had passed away; time and place of burial undetermined.

On a hunch I called Hillside Cemetery in Inglewood. It was an exclusive and exclusively Jewish cemetery not far from Brentwood. They were holding a service, and he'd be interred in a vault.

Thanking the receptionist, I hung up and dialed Parisian's to order a wreath.

"Mrs. Parisian, would you have the following written across the ribbon: 'Rest in Peace, Uncle Mickey'? And, Mrs. Parisian, would you do me a favor? I'm going to send along a card. But if anyone wants to know who sent the wreath, would you please promise me to say you don't know?"

This time I paid full price.

• • •

Meyer Harris Cohen died a sick old man, stripped of his wealth and his power. All the things the little illiterate paperboy from Boyle Heights in east L.A. had dreamed of becoming were only memories—a few photos, strips of film, and words. Most of his "boys" were either dead or serving prison sentences.

He'd been called many things—"a scrappy welterweight boxer," "a tough street hood," "a stickup and knockover gangster," "a cold-blooded killer," "Hollywood Mob Boss," "socio-path"—and those things he was, but the title that lasted the longest, endured the acid test of time, and wrote itself large on the enduring legend of Hollywood fit him best of all.

And good or bad, it's what he'll always be to me.

King of the Sunset Strip.

AFTERWORD

Many people, living and deceased, are mentioned in this book. Among those are our classmates and schoolmates from Hollywood Professional School. This wonderful, eccentric Hollywood institution—which functioned as a preparatory academy for children in kindergarten through high school who were either in or planned on entering the world of entertainment—closed its doors on Hollywood Boulevard forever in 1985.

Many of us have remained both close friends and colleagues over the decades since we graduated, and our lives have intertwined as our careers in Hollywood, entertainment, and the arts have carried us over an ever-changing cultural and artistic terrain. Our informal social/car club, Big Bertha's Riders, named irreverently for the school's headmistress/principal, survived and still on occasion "rallys."

Since each person mentioned played a part in Steve's story, we thought we'd honor their contributions as actors and actresses in this real-life drama. What follows is our cast, in order of appearance.

ROLL CREDITS

Marlene Willis (deceased)

Bobby Driscoll (deceased)

Steven Benson

Anthony Mazzola (deceased)

Annette Funicello

Sandra Dee

David Carlson

Joanne Grauer, D.D.

Jock Putnam Carter

Les Weingard (deceased)

Matteo Muti, Ph.D.

Don Durran (deceased)

Larry Beckstead

Tommy Cole

Connie Stevens

Sandy Ferra

Fred Donn Jr.

Vernette and Melantha Tatum

Mark Cavell (deceased)

Major Goddard, HPS drama
    coach (deceased)

Lauri and Larry Collins

ABOUT THE AUTHORS

Steve Stevens has been in show business for more than fifty years, as an actor, producer, casting director, and for more than thirty years a Screen Actors Guild franchised talent agent. He is the author of *So You Want to Be in Show Business.* He lives in Chatsworth, California. **Craig Lockwood** is an award-winning columnist, correspondent, photographer, and author. He has also written for the theater and for television. He lives in Laguna Beach, California.